# Artists Labour Market, Cultural Policy and Creative Economy

Focusing on artists and creators, this shortform book analyses the labour market in the creative economy in the context of cultural policies.

Based on a series of studies involving Polish artists spanning 10 years, the book identifies the key factors needed to understand contemporary labour markets in the creative and cultural sectors worldwide. The authors integrate artists' perspectives to present truly rounded evidence, shedding light on the applicational perspective of the research findings.

Illuminating the socioeconomic status of artists in Poland, this book is essential reading for researchers interested in cultural policy and the creative economy, as well as work and labour studies more broadly. It will also be of interest to practitioners in the creative and cultural industries.

**Dorota Ilczuk** is an ordinary professor and economist working at the Faculty of Humanities, and the Head of The Creative Economy Research Centre at SWPS University, Poland.

**Anna Karpińska** is a cultural researcher and PhD candidate at SWPS University Poland, with research interests in the fine arts and labour market of artists and creators.

**Emilia Cholewicka** is a cultural economist, an assistant professor at SWPS University, Poland, and a dancer, with research interests in dance and women in the labour market.

# Routledge Focus on Economics and Finance

The fields of economics are constantly expanding and evolving. This growth presents challenges for readers trying to keep up with the latest important insights. Routledge Focus on Economics and Finance presents short books on the latest big topics, linking in with the most cutting-edge economics research.

Individually, each title in the series provides coverage of a key academic topic, whilst collectively the series forms a comprehensive collection across the whole spectrum of economics.

**The Economics of ObamaCare**
*Łukasz Jasiński*

**Monetary Policy and Inflation**
Quantity Theory of Money
*Mateusz Machaj*

**Customer Data Sharing Frameworks**
Twelve Lessons for the World
*Anton Didenko, Natalia Jevglevskaja and Ross P. Buckley*

**Crowdfunding European Business**
*Antonella Francesca Cicchiello*

**The Chief Financial Officer and Corporate Performance**
Finance, Governance and Risk
*Elżbieta Bukalska, Anna Wawryszuk-Misztal and Tomasz Sosnowski*

**Artists Labour Market, Cultural Policy and Creative Economy**
A Triangular Model in Poland
*Dorota Ilczuk, Anna Karpińska and Emilia Cholewicka*

For more information about this series, please visit: www.routledge.com/ Routledge-Focus-on-Economics-and-Finance/book-series/RFEF

# Artists Labour Market, Cultural Policy and Creative Economy

A Triangular Model in Poland

**Dorota Ilczuk, Anna Karpińska and Emilia Cholewicka**

Routledge
Taylor & Francis Group

LONDON AND NEW YORK

First published 2024
by Routledge
4 Park Square, Milton Park, Abingdon, Oxon OX14 4RN

and by Routledge
605 Third Avenue, New York, NY 10158

*Routledge is an imprint of the Taylor & Francis Group, an informa
business*

*British Library Cataloguing-in-Publication Data*
A catalogue record for this book is available from the British Library

ISBN: 978-1-032-51083-5 (hbk)
ISBN: 978-1-032-51085-9 (pbk)
ISBN: 978-1-003-40103-2 (ebk)

DOI: 10.4324/9781003401032

Typeset in Times New Roman
by MPS Limited, Dehradun

# Contents

# Introduction

## Context

In 2012, artists in Poland went on strike. Shortly thereafter, the strike soon became symbolised by a picture of the well-known artist Zbigniew Libera, who had been photographed with a sign reading 'I am an artist, but that does not mean I work for free.' That grassroots protest initiated a discussion about what the work of artists is. The debate was also prompted by the fact that the strike was supported by the non-profit organisation Civic Forum for Contemporary Art, which called for the 'creation of a system that will not put artists on the margins of society!' and urged 'the government to start talking with artists!' It should be recalled that in 2023 US screenwriters affiliated with the Writers Guild of America (WGA) have gone on strike, too. They accused studios/platforms such as Netflix, Amazon, Apple, Disney, Paramount and Sony of creating an environment of exploitation in which screenwriting assignments are outsourced to freelancers and people on so-called 'junk' contracts, thereby avoiding the costs associated with actual remuneration. They were also calling for regulation of the use of artificial intelligence in artistic processes. Screenwriters have been joined by Hollywood actors with similar demands. The consequences of the strike included cancelled productions and the absence of artists at promotional events and festivals. But what was actually at stake? Especially as these two examples are not isolated. It turns out that not only Polish or American artists have striven for a better or rather decent living. Artists are often expected to work for free, or they receive very low remuneration. Artistic activity includes irregular revenue resulting from idle time in creative work. One often hears about the exorbitant earnings of artists, but this applies only to a strictly limited group of 'stars' (Rosen 1981; Ilczuk 2020). In fact, most creators do not earn income that would guarantee them social security.

What contributes to this situation? Firstly, the work of the artist is not properly appreciated. Somewhere, the understanding of artistic work as labour is slipping away, and the romantic myth of the poor brilliant artist who does not deserve financial appreciation during his lifetime prevails.

DOI: 10.4324/9781003401032-1

Secondly, the level of general cultural education influencing the creation of cultural competencies in societies is too low. Furthermore, the cultural policy pursued in European countries (welfare state model) seems to be failing. The focus on institutions and programmes ignores the situation of artists and creators themselves, and the scope of programmes dedicated to artists is too narrow to influence the level of income earned by them. To add to this, the legislation that is supposed to protect the rights of authors arising from the practice of creation is struggling to keep up with the new digitalised reality. A glaring example at the moment is the issue of legal protection of creations used by artificial intelligence. Despite the efforts of UNESCO (1980) and the European Parlament (2007), the status of the artist, rather than a remedy for the alarmingly difficult socio-economic situation of this group, is still an unresolved problem.

This is an anomalous issue, as all this is happening at a time when culture has been recognised as a source of both cultural, social and economic development. A new context of the role of culture has been specifically created with the emergence of the term 'creative economy' coined to emphasise the much larger area in which cultural goods and services are produced: traditional culture is placed here along with the cultural and creative industries. This area should be supported wisely. It is crucial, as it translates not only into economic growth (Deloitte report 2021) but also general social well-being. It should be also highlighted that the work of artists and creators is a key factor in the development of various sectors of the creative economy (the so-called cultural and creative sectors, i.e. CCS). Shaping cultural policy in the 21st century requires taking into account not only the imperative of innovation and socio-economic changes or the development of a digital society, but also ensuring decent working conditions for all those employed at CCS, including artists and creators.

Wise cultural policy requires a decent research base. The scope of actions taken to monitor, analyse and support factors contributing to the development of the CCS is still too limited when compared to others. These shortcomings are closely connected with the need for carrying out research into different aspects of the CCS. There is a particular research gap in the area of correlations between the creative economy, cultural policies and the artists' labour market: this blank sphere warrants an in-depth, coherent analysis and monitoring displayed in this book. Emerging studies presented, on the artists' labour market and the creative economy, are therefore of particular applied interest to cultural policy representatives, but not only. This area addresses specific issues that correspond to the rigours of the needs of cultural economics professionals – both students and researchers. On the other hand, the book can be of interest to a wide audience, given the growing importance of cultural work and the creative economy in the global economic arena.

**Research scope, objectives and method**

Let us begin by saying that this is not a scientific book like the others – presenting the results of desk research and field studies carried out with more or less flair. This time, it is an in-depth multidisciplinary analysis based on the results of a series of studies carried out successively and sequentially over ten years, under the guidance of the same person. In addition, the research has a strong applied character, having already become part of the creation of Poland's cultural policy. This book, therefore, is the result of a critical analysis of what has been achieved empirically, cognitively and applicationally to present a tangible picture of the artists' labour market. This picture was painted, or rather constructed from various perspectives, by different teams under the direction of Professor Dorota Ilczuk. Hence, this makes it extremely rich and varied, but also consistently realised. This richness of results is, on the one hand, a huge cognitive advantage, but on the other hand, it has been an analytical challenge for the authors of this book – to create a new, as complete as possible problematic collage presented here – touching on the artists' labour market, but also on the creative economy and cultural policy – from a new perspective, with new knowledge and in a constantly changing reality.

What should be emphasised, therefore, is that an important aim of this book is to analyse creative economics and cultural policies in a broader scientific context and to present a single story to an international audience in the form of a book showing the results of research derived from a whole series of studies on the artists' labour market conducted over ten years in Poland by Ilczuk. However, while the Polish artists' strike in 2012 was the first impulse for this massive series of research in the area of the artists' labour market, initiated by Ilczuk, it was not the only reason. The investigation was also stimulated by the new cultural and socio-economic role of culture, and, as a result, the new presence of the artist and creator, especially from the professional perspective. This new perspective was recently developed mostly within cultural economics. All studies were carried out at the SWPS University,[1] Poland, and from 2019 at the Creative Economy Research Centre at SWPS University. The other two book co-authors also situated at the SWPS University – Emilia Cholewicka, PhD, and Anna Karpińska were actively involved in the implementation of Ilczuk's study especially in its qualitative and quantitative field research, but also accompanying the development of the topic in their areas of expertise: dance, ballet and the role of women, as well as visual arts and the art market.

What is more, there are also two research aims of the book, which we would like to introduce more precisely. The first one is purely cognitive or scientific, whereas the second one endeavours to show how to implement research findings within public policy formation.

The first research aim was to carry out an in-depth analysis of determinants of the development of the labour markets of artists and creators, considering both the question of supply and demand. We also attempted to indicate the strength of connections between the creative economy and the artists' labour markets, particularly those related to research and cultural policy.

The second research aim, which we refer to as applicative or implementation-oriented, was to indicate the difficult way of implementing research findings about the labour market of artists and creators, or, speaking more broadly, about cultural economics in the cultural policy of Poland.

Going further, the process of analysis presented in this book was based on verifying the three hypotheses, which refer to the situation in Poland; however, it does not mean that they lack any universal meaning that could be applied to contexts outside Poland.

The first hypothesis was both a point of departure and a reference spot, accompanying us in the whole research process that took place between 2013 and 2022, and it reads as follows:

*The professional situation of artists and creators is not adequate to the observed tendencies of development, according to which culture and its industries have been considered a significant component of the creative economy, and accordingly, a new area of investment, a source of creativity and innovation.*

A further two hypotheses were formulated in the course of the comprehensive analytical process. They are the linkage of the research touching upon the labour market for artists and creators, creative economy as well as cultural policy:

*Influencing both the supply and demand side of the labour market of artists and creators by means of instruments of support offered by the state, local authorities, non-governmental and private institutions contributes to greater growth of the creative economy.*

These were accompanied by a third one, which reads:

*Insufficient monitoring and analysis of the situation within artists' and creators' labour markets aggravates the difficult socio-economic situation of artists and creators, as well as prevents systemic support from functioning properly.*

In order to meet the research aims and to verify the hypotheses, a number of research undertakings were specified. They included the following:

- determining the role of artists' work in the development of the creative economy at the current stage of digitalization of the global economy
- conceptualising the labour market of artists and creators, or identifying the specifics of the labour market of artists and creators
- carrying out an analysis of the international situation of labour markets of artists, with a focus placed on forms of public support used in various countries
- diagnosing the social and economic situation of artists in Poland
- estimating the population size of the community of artists, creators and performers in Poland (which was a pioneering research investigation)
- demonstrating (in)equalities among male and female artists in Poland
- describing the situation of theatre artists in the time of the COVID-19 pandemic
- creating an original concept of a system supporting artists, creators and performers
- analysing the process of applying research findings about the labour market of artists, which was exemplified by the work on the act on the professional artist.

In the course of meeting the objectives, general and global speculations were illustrated by examples taken from a wide international perspective, with a special focus on the situation in Poland. It should be noted that the research encompassed practically all fields of the arts, along with the cultural and creative industries.

The research analysis process included methods and techniques from the paradigm of social sciences and humanities. The plethora of research methods and the interdisciplinary character of the approach are typical of cultural economics – a scientific discipline which serves as a theoretical framework for the research, thanks to its particular usefulness in this kind of investigation aimed at examining the artists' labour market and the creative economy. Therefore, during previous research, the quantitative and qualitative studies were conducted, following an in-depth and thorough analysis of the secondary data. Various methods, ranging from observation, a critical analysis of the literature on the subject, questionnaire surveys and case study analyses, statistical methods, the monographic method and the analysis and logical construction of interviews were employed. In addition, for the sake of the research, we employed our original methods as well. We are currently subjecting all results to a secondary, critical analysis, which forms the basis of this book. The specific competence of our work was the ability to analyse and selectively choose the rich and wide-ranging results of artists' labour market surveys conducted at different times and in different ways. This was tricky and challenging work due to the different nature of the involvement of the three authors in the series of studies carried out between 2012 and 2022. Particularly for the head of operations – Dorota Ilczuk, who was uninterruptedly in the supervisor position.

**Series of research into the labour market of artists and creators between 2012 and 2022**

Ilczuk began her research series on the labour markets of artists and creators by recognising the general specifics of artistic work, along with the situation of Polish artists, creators and performers (2013). The next research undertaking was to investigate the international perspective of the labour market of artists, with special reference to the support they receive (2017). Following these findings, Ilczuk ran works on the creation of an original concept of a system of support for artists in Poland, which became part of the general debate in Poland about the status of the artist (2017). It was a drive for the next great research project run by Ilczuk, commissioned by the Fryderyk Chopin National Institute, which served as the basis for estimating the costs of the future proposal of a new act on the professional artist in Poland. It was in 2018 when the team led by Ilczuk for the first time in modern Poland estimated the population size of the professional community of artists, creators and performers in Poland. In 2020, Ilczuk together with her team were commissioned by the Zbigniew Raszewski Theatre Institute to carry out research into the social and economic situation of theatre artists during the COVID-19 pandemic. The subsequent research projects were meant to evaluate the brand image of the Polish Society of Authors (ZAiKS), which is the largest Polish organisation of collective management (2022). Currently, in 2023, following a commission from Music Export Poland, the research team under Ilczuk's supervision is investigating value chains within the pop music sector in Poland. Moreover, she was supervising the doctoral dissertation written by Emilia Cholewicka which broadened the area of expertise concerning women in the ballet labour market (2023) and is partially discussed in this book.

It is important to emphasise that the publications with outcomes of those investigations are available mainly in Polish. The first publication was published almost a decade ago. *SOSART. Study of the labour market of artists and creators in Poland* (Dudzik and Ilczuk 2013) is a scholarly response to the so-called SOS sign sent by underpaid artists in Poland at the beginning of the second decade of the 21st century. In 2015, the monograph *Artyści na rynku pracy* (Ilczuk, Dudzik and Jeran 2015) was published by Ilczuk, Dudzik, Gruszka and Jeran. This was the first comprehensive monograph in Poland to shed light on the specifics of artistic work. Afterwards, in 2018 an article by Ilczuk and Karpińska, emphasising the lack of systematic solutions for artists in Poland was published in English, although in a Polish economic journal, under the title *The Labour Market of Artists. Free, But Not Wild* (Ilczuk and Karpińska, 2018). Moreover, this article looked at support schemes for artists in other countries and introduced the financial situation of artists in chosen countries.

The outcomes of the revolutionary research on the size of artists' population have been published in the monograph *Policzone i policzeni. Artyści i artystki w Polsce* (Ilczuk et al. 2020). Since the project's inception, the related publications have attracted great attention among scholars, students, artists, as well as cultural-policy representatives in Poland.

Of course, each project was completed with an internal report outlining the findings that were available online. These reports had a limited readership because of their work-in-progress character.

Figure 0.1 demonstrates the timeline of the extensive process of investigation that Ilczuk undertook beginning a decade ago and continuing up to the present day.

**The structure of this book**

The structure of this book corresponds to its aims and research hypotheses.

**The introduction** contains a general context of the book topic and the specific nature of the analysis carried out in it. An outline of the main objectives of the book, the hypotheses and the research methods are presented sequentially. In addition, one will find the structure of the book, acknowledgements and a note from the authors placed at the end. The problems signalled in the introduction are discussed in detail in the following chapters, presenting subsequent research projects along with their findings.

**Chapter 1** is the theoretical introduction to the monograph. It describes the theoretical basis of connections between the creative economy and the labour market of artists and creators. It presents the necessary definitions and information about the labour market of artists and creators, as well as discusses its specific features. Likewise, it also presents the issue of monitoring and analysis of the artists' labour market, along with an outline of the research projects that Ilczuk carried out and used as a basis for the analyses presented.

**Chapter 2** analyses the labour markets of artists and creators in selected countries, such as South Korea, Australia, Great Britain, Lithuania or the Netherlands, according to criteria which have been of interest to researchers and public authorities responsible for the implementation of cultural policies and also artists themselves, i.e. criteria which pertains to the labour market of artists with regard to their socio-economic situation. This chapter sets out the specific features of the labour markets of

LABOUR MARKET OF
ARTISTS AND CREATORS
IN POLAND

Pro Cultura Foundation.
WSG in Bydgoszcz, SWPS University

**2013**

SUPPORT FOR CREATORS AND
ARTISTS. INTERNATIONAL
PERSPECTIVE

SWPS University for the Polish
National Conference on Culture (OKK)

**2017**

CULTURAL REFORM:
EXPERTISE PACKAGE

Creative Economy Research Center
of the SWPS University for the OKK

**2017**

ESTIMATION OF THE NUMBER
OF ARTISTS, CREATORS AND
PERFORMERS IN POLAND

Creative Economy Research
Center of the SWPS University

**2018**

THEATRE ARTISTS DURING
COVID-19 PANDEMIC

Creative Economy Research
Center of the SWPS University

**2020**

BRAND IMAGE OF THE
SOCIETY OF AUTHORS ZAIKS

Creative Economy Research
Center of the SWPS University

**2022**

HOMO SALTATRIX: THE SITUATION
OF WOMEN ON LABOUR MARKET
OF BALLET ARTISTS

Doctoral dissertation by Emilia Cholewicka
Supervisors: Dorota Ilczuk, Sandra Frydrysiak

**2023**

*Figure 0.1* The timeline of Dorota Ilczuk's research projects.
*Source:* own work.

artists and creators, which are different because of certain geographical features, as demonstrated by the analysis of secondary sources. The chapter presents a systematised outline of various solutions, programmes, institutions and mechanisms used in the analysed countries to support artists, creators and performers.

**Chapter 3** presents the effects of the first research attempt to detect the professional situation of artists. The results come from the project conducted in Warsaw and Bydgoszcz in the year 2013. It shows the results of the survey and the FGI undertaken with the artists' employers – managers, producers, etc.

**Chapter 4** is focused on the general survey carried out across the whole of Poland to investigate the socio-economic situation of artists and creators 5 years later – in 2018, after the first attempt described in the previous chapter. The significance of the findings may be illustrated by the sample that participated in the project, which was representative enough to draw conclusions that refer to the whole population under scrutiny.

**Chapter 5** illustrates specific aspects of the labour market of artists. Section 5.1 focuses on the differences between women and men across artistic professions, addressing topics related to gender equality, including the gender pay gap, education or the length of professional activity time. Section 5.2 focuses on the situation of theatre artists in the times of the COVID-19 pandemic. Apart from musicians, it was one of the groups most affected by pandemic restrictions.

**Chapter 6** shows the methodology and findings of the ground-breaking research study that allowed us to estimate the number of artists and creators in Poland. The chapter presents each step of the research process and the circumstances in which it was carried out. The findings include first and foremost the total number of artists across various artistic industries and professions, as well as the mysterious multi-professional index relevant to this group, the determination of which was crucial in the estimation process.

**Chapter 7** This chapter is devoted to cultural policies. It shows the path from the research to the implementation of the results. In Section 7.1, we present a proposal for a support system for artists and creators, based on Ilczuk's research. The idea of creating a support system initiated a debate in the artistic community. That led to ground-breaking research that allowed us to estimate the number of artists and creators in Poland. This chapter describes how important Ilczuk's research has become in introducing real changes and developing solutions to support artists, including the act on the rights of the professional artist, currently being created in Poland.

The final part of the book, **Conclusions**, presents the most important reflections coming from the analytical work done by three authors. This book has shown the effects of the research in the scope of the socio-economic professional situation of artists, the creative economy and its embeddedness in cultural policy. The final part places a special focus on one significant outcome stemming from the analysis of the whole research process, i.e. the triangular model: the artists' labour market – creative sectors – cultural policy, which we have considered an added value in terms of investigating this area of scientific interest and a new method of analysis.

## Acknowledgements

We would like to express our sincere gratitude to the members of all research teams, who were involved in the implementation process of the research studies presented in this monograph. Firstly, we would like to thank the co-authors of the publications and research reports that have been carefully quoted in this book: Madga Dudzik, Ewa Gruszka-Dobrzyńska, Agnieszka Jeran, Wojciech Hazanowicz, Antoni Roso-chacki, Ziemowit Socha, Sylwia Stano-Strzałkowska, as well as the current members and associates working at the Creative Economy Research Centre, especially Maciej Kozieł, who offered technical support to the authors in the final stage of book preparation. Whilst writing, we used extracts of our earlier publications: there are relevant in-text citations indicating the original sources. The extracts were used in different contexts and interpreted differently compared to the source material.

## Authors' note

Who are WE in that book? WE the three authors of this book. Prof. Dorota Ilczuk is the pioneer figure on cultural economics in Poland and a leading researcher on the labour market of artists. Emilia Cholewicka, PhD and Anna Karpińska, PhD candidate, two young researchers, both cultural economists with research interests in the markets covering dance and the fine arts. All we are connected with the CBnGK at the SWPS University, the first privately-owned university in Poland. We are a committed team, always dedicated to the task at hand.

*We are full of research passion, but also feel strongly the need to change the situation of artists ... and for the better. Likewise, we maintain that the artistic labour markets should be FREE, BUT NOT A FREE-FOR-ALL.*

*DI, ECH, AK cultural economists*

## Note

1 The SWPS University has undergone two important name changes. These changes reflected the growing importance of the university, which was 'climbing' up the academic ladder. At first, it was called the Warsaw School of Social Psychology (SWPS). In 2015, SWPS became the first non-public university in Poland and changed its name to the SWPS University of Social Sciences and Humanities. Finally, in 2023, the name changed to the SWPS University and this term will be used in this monograph.

# References

Deloitte. (2021). The Future of the Creative Economy A report by Deloitte. Retrieved from https://www2.deloitte.com/content/dam/Deloitte/uk/Documents/technology-media-telecommunications/deloitte-uk-future-creative-economy-report-final.pdf

Dudzik, T. M., & Ilczuk, D. (2013). Sosart. Study on the labour market of artists and creators in Poland. Report. Pro-Cultura.

European Parlament. (2007). Resolution of 7 June 2007 on the social status of artists (2006/2249(INI)). https://www.europarl.europa.eu/doceo/document/TA-6-2007-0236_EN.html

Ilczuk, D., & Karpińska, A. (2018). The labour market of artists. Free, but not wild. Edukacja Ekonomistów i Menedżerów, *50*(4), 159–170.

Ilczuk, D., Dudzik, T., Gruszka, E., & Jeran, A. (2015). Artyści na rynku pracy. Wydawnictwo Attyka.

Ilczuk, D., Gruszka-Dobrzyńska, E., Socha, Z., & Hazanowicz W. (2020). Policzone i policzeni! Artyści i artystki w Polsce. *Wydawnictwo Uniwersytetu SWPS – Dom Wydawniczy Elipsa*, Warszawa.

Rosen, S. (1981). The economics of superstars. The American Economic Review, *71*(5), 845–858.

United Nations Educational, Scientific and Cultural Organization (UNESCO). (1980). 1980 RECOMMENDATION CONCERNING THE STATUS OF THE ARTIST. United Nations Educational, Scientific and Cultural Organization (UNESCO). Retrieved from: https://en.unesco.org/about-us/legal-affairs/recommendation-concerning-status-artist

# 1 Labour market of artists and creators in the creative economy

## 1.1 Artistic work in the development of the creative economy

The first works of art, including rock drawings or the figurine of Venus with her wide hips and full breasts, were created in the Palaeolithic Age. It is no lie, then, to say that art has accompanied humans for millennia. This, in turn, means that even in primitive societies there were remarkably gifted individuals, possessing skills and talents that would allow them to perform artistic work. Marian Golka, a Polish sociologist of culture, assumes that in ancient history, artists would be commissioned by tribal chiefs or priests based on some specific type of patronage. However, their remuneration did not have any market value, for in primitive societies people did not use money.

Church and secular patronage developed and became more powerful in the Middle Ages and the Renaissance. The relationship between artists and their patrons had a significant influence on artistic practices. The task of the creator was to fulfil the wishes of the client, who would even frequently determine the price of the work. The artistic process would be initiated not because of the artist's needs or some kind of inspiration, but rather because of a contract that set out, often in very precise terms, the conditions for the execution of the work, its purpose and its recipients (Golka 1991).

The relationship between artist and patron would become more casual over time. Artists started to create works of art and store them for future use or viewing, i.e. without having a predetermined buyer. This allowed them to enjoy more creative freedom and become independent from patrons. At the same time, prospering artists were not able to meet the needs of all of their clients, which led to the development of artistic workshops, where qualified artist-craftsmen had a specific task to do. There was also the hierarchy of a guild: basic tasks were performed by journeymen. There were also individuals, educated in the workshop, who cooperated with artists; and who would then become independent and open their own workshops.

DOI: 10.4324/9781003401032-2

It becomes clear, then, that artistic work was often a result of teamwork. An image of a genius artist working alone is actually a romantic vision of artistic work founded on the belief held by Michelangelo about the divine element which only a true artist can extract from matter (Dworzak 2013). Over time, both the person of an artist and artistic work became associated with specific images which we still use today. This may be illustrated by the common belief that an artist is someone who is above average, able to experience the world more deeply and strongly; someone unique and atypical, whose work and talent are great gifts of fate. Such images influenced the discourse about artistic work. For a long time, there was no debate about the socio-economic situation of artists, since it did not match the image of artistic work, which was pictured as being almost sacred. However, soon artists and their work began to appear more and more often in academic discourse.

The approach to creative and artistic activity in the economy shaped during the Industrial Revolution proved to be especially persistent. Adam Smith described artistic labour as that area of activity which did not contribute to producing the wealth of a nation (Smith 1937); throughout the whole 20th century, the belief that this kind of activity was costly for the economy (Baumol 1966) and did not produce any measurable effects became more and more popular. It was at the end of the 20th century that the approach changed (see e.g. Throsby 2010, Ilczuk 2012), which proved how wrong Smith was. Indeed, culture and its funding should be viewed from a broader perspective. Funding culture means an investment in economic growth and the development of the labour market. It is also a foundation for social education and a tool of social policy, used in favour of social cohesion. It is a sector of the economy that has yielded positive external results, which by definition are hard to measure. What is more, since the 1990s, research on cultural participation has proven that a major portion of spending on culture, and of time devoted to culture, is actually devoted to the consumption of goods and services that are industrially produced. It has been observed that cultural life depends not only on works created within fields that are traditionally considered part of culture, but it is also increasingly influenced by the cultural and creative industries. A modern approach to culture, and its social and economic significance, requires recognising that these two areas mutually shape cultural life. Accordingly, in the literature on the subject, a new term for the creative economy has emerged, one that emphasises the intellectual and creative component in the production of symbolic goods and cultural goods, and indicates a much greater area in which these goods are produced: traditional culture is thus perceived together with the cultural and creative industries (Ilczuk 2012, Throsby 2010).

The concept of the creative economy was presented by John Howkins in 2001 in his work with the meaningful title *The Creative Economy. How*

*People Make Money from Ideas* (2002). The concept is based on indicating the correlations between the economy, culture, new technologies and creativity. It combined and unified various concepts, including the concept of a creative class, creative cities, cultural industries, creative sectors and different types of creativity. Howkins observed that creativity *per se* is not a form of activity, but can become its foundation when an idea is born or a product that may be sold is created. The key moment of transition between abstraction and reality, or from an idea to a product, is difficult to observe because creative processes take place in a non-standard way. The economy and creativity cannot be perceived separately, since the relations between them create newer and newer networks and unique values. What is more, combining the economy, culture, creativity and technology has a positive impact, since it generates new jobs, and stimulates economic growth and innovation. This is how the term of the creative economy was created, a term that encompasses all goods and services that fall under the provisions of copyright and related rights (including patent law) (Howkins 2002).

Though Howkins provides a list of the key sectors of the creative economy, including research and development (R&D), publishing, software, television and radio, design, music (the phonographic industry), film (the cinematographic industry), toys and games production, advertising, architecture, performing arts, arts and crafts, video games, fashion and visual arts, he perceives the creative economy from a much broader perspective. The concept includes those sectors (irrespective of whether they have a cultural or digital component) which are subject to intellectual property law. For instance, science is recognised as part of the creative economy, since its products are protected by copyright and patent law. Still, the question of whether a specific industry is part of the creative economy depends somehow on the significant share of artistic and creative work.

It was, however, the UNCTAD, a specialised organisation within the UN, that published a report under the title *Creative Economy Report 2008: The Challenge of Assessing the Creative Economy: Towards Informed Policy-Making* (UNCTAD 2008), which introduced the concept of the creative economy to the global academic discourse. The report provides a definition of the creative industries, which, accordingly, use intellectual capital and creativity as a basis for creating, producing and distributing goods and services. What is important is that these industries include countable products as well as artistic and intellectual work, which is difficult to measure quantitatively. They are also a dynamically developing area of trade. The significance of the creative economy is constantly growing and it has been highlighted that in addition to promoting social inclusion, cultural diversity and human development, the creative economy has the potential to determine economic growth.

It is worth mentioning here that the introduction of the term 'creative economy' into academic discourse has sparked a debate about the terminology used in this context. At first, scholars talked about the creative industries, but the nomenclature did not fit the non-industry sectors, such as dance or painting. Finally, in 2022, the collective term 'the cultural and creative sectors' (CCS), or simply sectors of the creative economy, was accepted because the word 'sectors' includes both industries and non-industries.

Is the creative economy really such a 'new phenomenon'? According to John Newbigin, the author of the report, *Creative Economy: An Introductory Guide* for British Council, 'creative economy' is a term derived from the cultural industries, which are 'as old as human society' (Newbigin 2010: 13). He writes that:

> Digital media and hundreds of thousands of creative enterprises that have been made possible by digital technologies are, of course, new. So are many of the goods and services that an increasingly sophisticated global market demands. But the desire to create things whose value is not purely practical – things that are beautiful; that communicate cultural value through music, drama, entertainment and the visual arts; that communicate social position through style and fashion – these desires are as old as human society. There always have been, and always will be, people with the imagination and talent to make and do these things. And there will always be people who are prepared to pay them to do it. That is the basis of the creative economy. (Newbigin 2010: 13)

David Throsby in his 2000 book *Economics and Culture* defines the cultural industries as the ones that produce cultural goods within the arts, such as film, theatre or literature. Products of the cultural industries are characterised by an impact greater than the one observed in the case of individually produced goods. What is more, more employees are involved in the process of the production of cultural goods. In addition to producing cultural goods and making them accessible, another basic function of the cultural industries consists of creating jobs and developing the intellectual potential of societies.

A classification and hierarchy of sectors of the creative economy was put forward in 2006 by the KEA European Affairs team, led by Philippe Kern. They prepared the report *The Economy of Culture in Europe*, which had been authorised by the European Commission. The document presents the division into the cultural and creative sectors. The core part of the division is the non-industry sector, including the visual arts (painting, sculpture, photography), the performing arts (dance, theatre) and heritage (museums, archaeological sites, archives). Another circle comprises the cultural industries that produce goods on a mass scale, i.e. film and video, television and the radio, video games, music, books and the press. The next circle represents the creative industries, in particular design (including fashion), architecture and advertising. The peripheral circle, which is the most distant from the core, includes related industries, such as the production of mobile phones or computers. Kern does not include this circle in the calculation of the economic value of culture (KEA European Affairs 2006). This classification served as the basis for the typology of the creative economy sectors, created and introduced to academic discourse by David Throsby. In the paper *The Concentric Circles Model of the Cultural Industries* (2008), he systematised and elaborated on the division, presenting it in the form of a four-circle model. The first circle, which is a type of centre and source of creative ideas requiring the most creative work, includes core creative arts, i.e. literature, music, performing arts and visual arts. Another circle includes other core cultural industries, i.e. those industries that are directly and indirectly connected with culture: film, museums, galleries, libraries and photography. The term 'wider cultural industries' refers to heritage, books and other print media, sound recording, television and radio, as well as video and computer games. The last circle includes the so-called related industries, i.e. advertising, architecture, design and fashion, as well as tourism.

> Different goods have different degrees of cultural content relative to their commercial value; the model proposes that the more pronounced the cultural content of a particular good or service, the stronger is the claim of the industry producing it to be counted as a cultural industry. Thus are the concentric circles delineated: at the center are core industries whose proportion of cultural to commercial content is judged according to given criteria to be highest, with layers extending outwards from the center as the cultural content falls relative to the commercial value of the commodities or services produced. (Throsby 2008: 149)

It is worth noting that in the case of both Kern's and Throsby's classification, artistic work is the basis or the source of all the circles without which there would be no creative economy.

The most quoted idea presented by the author though is a much simpler conclusion: culture is a condition for economic growth. This statement follows from the theory of cultural goods, described by Throsby. He differentiates between economic behaviour, of which the aim is to achieve as much benefit as possible, and cultural behaviour, which has a collective nature. The consumption of cultural goods can happen collectively, but these goods also do not lose their value when they are used multiple times by various individuals. In order to refer to a product or service as a cultural good, three conditions need to be met. Firstly, creativity is required to produce the good; then, it must be protected by copyright; and finally, it has to convey symbolic meaning.

Dorota Ilczuk and Anna Karpińska write in their paper *Kultura jako koło zamachowe rozwoju gospodarki* that:

It happens that the economic value of a work of art is not very high, but the cultural value creates a situation in which this work is considered of a very high value. From the pragmatic point of view, it does not make sense. In practice, though, a collective experience of this kind, the use of a cultural good, especially if it is a product of high culture, makes this work of art a source of delight and an object of collective desire. (Ilczuk and Karpińska 2017: 129; translated by authors)

As argued by Bourdieu, objectified cultural capital, i.e. a product such as a work of art, is quite easily exchanged for economic and social capital. However, cultural capital occurs also in an institutional form (formal education) and an embodied one (human features), both of which are difficult to accumulate. Being able to recognise and value a cultural good translates directly into the social status and, quite frequently, also into the economic status of individuals. It may be assumed, then, that creating equal opportunities to access cultural capital would have a positive bearing on the limiting of social stratification. When differences between social groups start disappearing, social cohesion increases (Bourdieu 1986).

Despite this, even as recently as in 2006, when Philippe Kern with his team were creating his report *The Economy of Culture in Europe*, it was believed that culture and the economy were two separate areas with no common points. That belief resulted from the approach to culture and art understood as the sacred; and to the creative industries understood as the profane, that is connected only with pure entertainment as well as from ignoring the role of the cultural and creative sectors in economic growth. Still, if the economic dimension of these sectors was noticed, they were perceived rather as 'poor.' The reason for such an impression was, and still is, the bad financial situation of artists and high spending on public organisations. Kern set himself the goal of verifying this approach by measuring the profitability and productivity of the cultural and creative sectors. To this end, two indicators were chosen. Productivity means the ratio between value added and employment costs. This indicator shows how much value is generated for every euro spent on employment costs (wages, salaries, social costs). The survey showed that between 1999 and 2003, the sector of video games was developing fastest, reporting an increase from 1.32 to 1.66. The highest productivity indicator in 2003 was the one of the visual arts (2.04) as well as film and video (2.02). The second indicator was profitability, measured by the operating margin of companies active in the creative economy. This indicator shows what percentage of the turnover is retained after the operating costs have been deducted.

The highest profitability indicators in 2003 were the ones of design (10.5%), the visual arts (11.3%) as well as film and video (11.7%). Thanks to these indicators, it was proven that the cultural and creative sectors in Europe are as competitive as other industrial sectors; and in some cases, their results are even better. The creative sectors are developing faster than the rest of the economy if only thanks to being at the forefront of creating innovations and using technology. Accordingly, they offer more jobs, foster economic and social growth, and have a positive impact on social cohesion (KEA European Affairs 2006).

The most recent research has highlighted the economic dimension of the cultural and creative sectors to an even greater extent. The *CICERONE Creative Industries Cultural Economy Production Network* project, realised within the Horizon 2020 programme by the University of Amsterdam (NL), the SWPS University (PL), City, University of London (UK), University of Bari Aldo Moro (IT), University of Milano-Bicocca (IT), Stockholm University (SE), University of Barcelona (ES), University of Vienna (AT), Observatory of Cultural Economics (BG) and KEA European Affairs (BE), has a novel aim to investigate sectors of the creative economy by analysing production chains.

The CICERONE project website proposes the following:

To capture CCIs' simultaneously, local and global integration, the CICERONE project will apply the Global Production Network (GPN) approach. The GPN approach departs from the view that contemporary production processes are confined to one place and posits instead that production processes are integrated in complex networks which often comprise locations in a number of countries (Coe, 2015). Such an approach goes beyond traditional value-chain analyses by considering the organisational and spatial patterns of production networks as well as investigating the embeddedness of the various components in multi-scalar institutional regulatory contexts. It entails – among other things – examining the historical roots of local assets (notably the reproduction of specific skills); the power relationships between different actors; and the broader institutional and political setting on various spatial scales. To grasp the multifaceted nature of global production networks of EU-based CCIs, a multi-disciplinary framework which encompasses approaches using insights and methods from geography, sociological, economics, business studies, history and political science is needed. (CICERONE website)

To date, this approach has been applied mainly in the context of industries, such as car, electronic or clothes industries, to measure distributed manufacturing systems. The cultural and creative sectors are characterised by a strong focus on unique aesthetic values and, what is important, an almost infinite horizontal diversity (Caves 2000), unstable (inter-sector) cooperation and, most importantly, diversified forms of cooperation between a number of entities of different skills. The complexity of such undertakings requires coordination delivered by multidisciplinary teams, whereas production is subject to severe temporal constraints (Hobday 2000).

Some production chains in the cultural and creative sectors are different from typical global production networks. Instead of mass-producing a large number of similar products, we can observe the predominance of small companies choosing to focus on short, or even single, series of products. A show, a song or an album, a painting or a building design – all are unique products that are usually created by ad hoc production networks that vary across products (Power and Hallencreutz 2002; Power and Janson 2004; Pratt 2006).

In the project, it was assumed that the model for the production chain in the cultural and creative sectors consists of five stages: creation, production, distribution, exchange and archiving. The stage of creation usually distinguishes culture and its industries from other sectors of the economy. It is often based on intangible content or innovations, and the final product or service must meet the three conditions of a cultural good that Throsby wrote about. To a large extent, it is this stage when, as pillars of the cultural and creative sectors, artists engage, and their artistic work becomes a profession.

Before the crisis caused by the pandemic, the sectors of the creative economy had been flourishing, as indicated in the report of the OECD *The Culture Fix: Creative People, Places and Industries* from 2022. In terms of growth, the CCS outpaced the business economy by an average of six percentage points across the OECD countries (18% as against 12%). The same applied to employment growth in these sectors: an average of 13.4% compared to 9.1% in the OECD and EU countries, respectively. In 2020, in some countries, employment in the creative industries accounted for one in 20 jobs (OECD 2022). As indicated in the latest report *Re|Shaping Policies for Creativity* prepared by UNESCO, 10 million jobs have been lost globally in the creative economy sectors due to the COVID-19 pandemic. Although sectors of the creative economy account for 3.1% of global GDP and 6.2% of all employment, being at the same time one of the fastest growing sectors of the global economy, they are frequently overlooked by public or private investment (UNESCO, 2022). Of course, the impact of the pandemic has not been the same across all sectors. Those that included digital content (e.g. computer games, streaming) often did quite well. Nevertheless, sectors of the creative economy may be one of the sources of solutions to the crisis caused by the COVID-19 pandemic. Thanks to their innovative character, new product designs and production techniques, business models, and customer reach, they have fostered innovation across the whole economy. According to the analyses prepared by the OECD, 62% of employees in the creative economy sectors have completed higher education, and 40% work also in other sectors. It is thanks to them that innovations emerging in sectors of the creative economy have spread to other industries. Interestingly, professions in the creative economy are not at high risk of automation, which amounts to 10% as compared to 14% of the overall workforce (OECD 2022). This is a result of, for instance, the fact that these sectors are based on human creativity, innovation, talent and artistic work, all of which cannot be replaced by machines. Even the common use of artificial intelligence (AI), which can generate images based on issued guidelines, will not replace the artistic and creative work that is characterised by the creation of new solutions, which are often very surprising. Of course, not all employees in the creative economy sectors are artists – there are also, for instance, engineers, technicians, scientists or managers; but in this book we have decided to focus on the former.

## 1.2   Labour market of artists: overview and features

Let us start with a reflection on the economic significance of the labour market of artists, i.e. let's situate the concept in the terminological apparatus of economics: Economics is a social science concerned with the production, distribution, and consumption of goods and services (Nelson 2015). In other words, economics explains the process of allocating scarce resources between different, competing uses related to the unlimited needs and desires of individuals. Consumer goods and services (products), for whose acquisition we should have remuneration, have to be produced. To produce them, it is necessary to have production goods (or factors of production), which include natural resources (e.g. land, air) and human resources, i.e. work and capital (physical or financial). In the contemporary economy, the development is to a lesser extent determined by traditional factors of production, such as work, land or financial capital; instead, intellectual capital and innovation are becoming the key factors. Price competition gives way to quality competition, where emotions, impressions, experiences and flexibility to adapt services to the needs of the individual customer count for a great deal. This observation is very important because the research area we are interested in is related to sectors of the creative economy (CCS) which precisely draws on intellectual capital.

All goods, including consumption and production goods, can be objects of market exchange. The market, one of the fundamental concepts of economics, is defined as the process by which decisions about production and consumption are coordinated by price (Begg, Fischer and Dornbusch 1993: 48). In a free market economy, there is no place for state intervention: everything is apparently handled by the 'invisible hand of the market.' The concept of 'known for being known' is attributed to Adam Smith, the father of modern-day economics; although we will not find it in his seminal work *The Wealth of Nations*. It was derived from the following quote by Smith, 'It is not from the benevolence of the butcher, the brewer, or the baker that we expect our dinner, but from their regard to their own interest' (in Begg, Fischer and Dornbusch 1993: 48). These words are worth remembering even though in practice we are often dealing with mixed economies, where there are various examples of state interventionism. They are often seen as a compromise between the efficiency of a free-market economy and the welfare economy (O'Hara 2019, Samuelson 2010). In the case of labour markets, the scope of this interventionism is particularly significant, which explains why in this context we talk about imperfect markets.

As explained by Ilczuk, Dudzik, Gruszka and Jeran in the monograph *Artyści na rynku pracy* the labour market of artists and creators is considered an example of factor markets (Ilczuk et al. 2015). As is the case with a typical factor market, the labour market of artists and creators has its own specific features. Demand in this market is derivative, which means it depends on demand for products, for whose production these factors are used. The level of demand in the labour market of artists depends on the readiness to participate in cultural life (financed from sources of private citizens) and the degree of state involvement in financing 'the collective consumption' of cultural goods. There is also a widespread expectation that sectors of the creative economy will become a new way of creating jobs for artists. It is worth highlighting here that the cultural policy of a state aims to influence not only the demand side of the market. Direct and indirect methods of financing artists and infrastructure also allow for state intervention on the supply side of the market. The result of this intervention should be the establishment of institutions supporting the functioning of all labour market entities as an efficient system that gives a sense of security and is understandable to all its participants. Institutions are understood here as 'standards, regulations and procedures guaranteeing compliance with them; their main task is to reduce uncertainty for human interactions' (North in Garbicz and Golachowski 2012). Such institutions will lead to an imperfect market, but this imperfection should act for the benefit of all market participants.

The object of our interest is labour, i.e. a resource that is owned by artists and creators, thanks to which they can receive money to meet their needs either in the consumption goods market as consumers or in the production goods market as producers. The exchange of work for remuneration takes place in the labour market. We will analyse this market from the point of view of the decisions made by artists and creators, i.e. in this context we will primarily use microeconomic analysis. As is the case with economics, we will be looking for an explanation of the process of allocating the resource of work between various, competing uses. For instance, an artist, giving piano lessons, cannot at the same time practise or perform; but it is possible that by teaching children this artist receives higher revenue than while performing (Ilczuk et al., 2015).

It should be emphasised here that artists are present also on the product market, which is especially true for visual artists. But since this is a group with numerous freelancers, i.e. individuals who are their own employers, we will concentrate on the labour market (in the EU statistics, self-employed individuals are considered employers as well; Szaban 2013: 17). So in the labour market, artists represent the supply side (as employees if they want to receive remuneration for their work), but they also act as entrepreneurs and employers; and can create a demand for the work of others.

A characteristic feature of the supply side of the market is the low degree of substitution of artists' talents and skills by technology, which is related to the specific character of artistic work in the field of the performing arts; diagnosed in the so-called 'cost disease.' This phenomenon was observed and then described in *Performing Arts: The Economic Dilemma* by William Baumol and William G. Bowen published in 1966, one of the ground-breaking texts about the economic aspect of artistic work. Following their analysis of the financial situation of professional theatre companies, ballet troupes, opera companies and music groups in the USA, the researchers observed that artistic work is not influenced by technological development to the extent which is observable in other sectors of the economy. Instead of making the work of art cheaper, all technological innovations basically make its production more expensive. This is because labour productivity remains the same. As explained by Ilczuk in her book *Ekonomika kultury*:

> ... the production of the performing arts is characterised by a high and growing share of personnel costs. And the increase in personnel costs, which is not alleviated by the increase in labour productivity, leads to an increase in the unit cost of cultural production. All attempts made to increase labour productivity by means of cost cutting are connected with decreasing the quality/the level of the end product. (Ilczuk 2012: 29–30; translated by authors)

The cost disease phenomenon is still one of the reasons for state interventionism in the area of culture. An increase in the salaries of artists caused by inflation processes will lead to an increase in labour costs, which will in the end lead to a deficit, since production costs of a performance undercut any potential profits. So when personnel costs increase and this is not alleviated by an increase in labour productivity and the unit cost of cultural production is higher, then the profitability of an undertaking is potentially no longer cost-effective. A solution to this situation is either to stop the non-profitable operation or to find an additional source of financing, which may come from a patron or sponsor, or indeed the state budget. It does not mean, though, that artistic work does not result in profitable undertakings. The latter may be illustrated by numerous examples of activities and projects from sectors of the creative economy, which are aimed at generating profits.

All attempts made to increase labour productivity through cost-cutting are connected with decreasing the quality of the end product, whereas technological innovations not only *do not* reduce the costs of artistic production, but they make what is a costly process even more expensive. Because of the limited demand for cultural goods, their prices (unless they are made available to users free of charge) are usually kept at a lower level than the economic calculation would suggest. As a result, the production and distribution of cultural goods and services, which require high input, cannot be balanced with sales revenue, which is a phenomenon Baumol and Bowen defined as the income gap, and which may be explained as chronic underfunding.

Time has positively verified Baumol's theory. Of course, some factors can reduce the power of constraints resulting from the same (Throsby, 2001). The possibility of lowering the costs of artistic work is provided by technological development. Radio, television or Internet broadcasts of performances increase revenue without the necessity of lowering the production quality. The possibility of avoiding the cost disease, which affects the performing arts, may be illustrated by art festivals. As noted by Bruno Frey in his 1994 paper *The Economics of Music Festivals*, during music festivals there is the opportunity to lower costs thanks to the low costs of artistic labour in the summer season, work of volunteers and local communities often covering some expenses as well as the opportunity to increase financing thanks to the interest of sponsors and additional revenue from the sale of tickets or gadgets. General tendencies which see an increase in the demand for the performing arts are of course also helpful when it comes to dealing with the deficit-generating character of their production processes. These are all factors that positively complement Baumol's theory, without questioning it at the same time. From the perspective of time, this theory remains topical and the observations presented by Baumol and Bowen have drawn the attention of economists to the specific realities of the performing arts, which require high personnel costs; and also to the profile of artistic work, which is different from other types of work found in economic activity.

As early as in the second half of the 20th century, Baumol claimed that 'in the world of the performing arts crisis is a way of life' (Baumol and Bowen 1966: 3). Contemporary research on the labour market of artists (Ilczuk 2013, 2015, 2020; Throsby 2010) indicates that artists are rarely driven by economic rationality while making professional decisions. Throsby (2010) argues that artists do not necessarily intend to maximise their profits, which means that the final price may be of minor or even no significance when it comes to allocating resources.

A limited demand for cultural goods and services, the specifics of the costs of artistic work as explored by Baumol (1966), as well as the lack of objective criteria of an artistic work, with the buyer often being unable to differentiate between a product that is only a result of successful marketing and a work of a talented artist, are the main, though not the only, conditions that determine the financial situation of artists. Artists often perform work beyond the level of adequate remuneration or without enough remuneration to remain in the market; though on the other hand, in the case of extremely talented artists or those who have been successfully promoted, we can observe extremely high remuneration. The latter refers to the phenomenon of stars defined by Rosen (1981), i.e. the possibility of a very limited group of chosen individuals, who are audiences' favourites, having exorbitant remuneration.

Elberse uses a similar framework of description of this economic area when she examines the market of talented individuals in areas that require creativity, i.e. markets for creative talent. She refers to the economists Robert Frank and Philip Cook, who were the first to describe the phenomenon of markets, where the winner takes it all, i.e. winner-take-all-markets:

> Markets with these characteristics are "winner-take-all markets," a term popularized by the economists Robert Frank and Philip Cook. But as they explain in their book on the topic, a more fitting term might be "those-near-the-top-get-a-disproportionate-share markets." In these markets, the efforts of only a small number of people at the very top – the superstars – largely drive the value of what is produced. (Elberse 2013: 156)

Elsewhere, Throsby points to another phenomenon common to an exclusive group of artists and creators earning much more than the rest, i.e. the greater majority of representatives of this professional group. It concerns the presence of celebrities in culture, whose popularity is connected with the development of digitalisation and new technologies in the context of production costs. He argues that large-scale consumption of a given type of art helps to reduce the costs of adding more consumers, which makes access to this type of art much greater. One of the outcomes of this situation is the emergence of celebrities whose fame cannot be fully explained by their talent (Throsby 2010).

In 2015 in the monograph *Artyści na rynku pracy* Ilczuk, Dudzik, Gruszka and Jeran examined the labour market of artists and creators in Poland and indicated factors that stimulate growth in this market. *The factors were as follows (*Ilczuk et al. 2015, p. 21)*:*

- *introducing tools for stimulating demand for artists' work*
- *raising awareness of the high value of original artistic work*
- *introducing systematic solutions in the field of professional and social security for artists and creators, in particular, health insurance and old-age pension security*
- *increasing the possibility of educating Polish artists abroad*
- *introducing reforms in the Polish system of arts education by making education fit the reality of the labour market, introducing the require-ment of doing an artistic apprenticeship and promoting the acquisition of entrepreneurial skills and of a basic knowledge of economics, financing of cultural activities and intellectual property rights*
- *increasing access to information about scholarships and grants awarded by ministries and local governments to artistic and creative communities*
- *developing adequate skills of potential managers of artists*
- *stimulating actions taken by organisations of artists and creators and by non-governmental organisations*

These factors refer to both the supply and the demand side of the labour market of artists and creators in Poland, but their character is also universal.

## 1.3 Specifying the area of research (CCS) and defining artists and creators

Carrying out the research required indicating its area and specifying the definition of artists and creators used. The classification put forward by KEA European Affairs (2006) and elaborated on in research conducted by economists of culture, including Throsby, was the point of departure that determined potential research areas. These are sectors of the creative economy, i.e. the cultural and creative sectors (CCS). There are multiple definitions of the creative economy and ways of mapping the same, i.e. indicating industries and types of activities that it includes. The one that our research makes recourse to is connected with cultural capital, which combines non-industrial areas of culture (main fields of culture) with the cultural and creative industries. This understanding of the creative economy was used by Ilczuk in 'Ekonomika kultury' and underlines the significance of culture and its industries as a new area of investment, a source of creativity and innovation (Ilczuk 2012). The work of artists and creators is an intrinsic factor of growth for the cultural and creative industries. At the same time, the possibility of the monetisation of artists' work in a much broader area of the cultural and creative sectors is highlighted. In this case, broader areas mean the need to have competencies to work in commercial markets and, frequently, to acquire new skills.

Ilczuk points out that organisations and firms of the creative economy come from all three sectors of the economy: public, private and commercial. They are very diverse both in terms of size and potential and in terms of the adopted legal form of operation, including cultural institutions, companies, own business activity, foundations, associations or individuals (Ilczuk 2012). Artists and creators are often one of the links of the value chain: they work in large production teams, e.g. in film, visual arts or music. Such activities are based on human talent and skills. They have the potential to create well-being and contribute to the creation of new jobs, and their role in the economy is constantly growing. This is exemplified by a great many instances of empirical research, which makes these activities an object of interest in the area of both science and strategies for managing the country.

In the series of research on the labour market of artists, Ilczuk applied two approaches to defining the terms 'creator' and 'artist.' Firstly, the definition of 'a professional artist,' which had been positively verified earlier, served as the basis. The definition was introduced by Throsby in his research on the labour market of artists and creators in Australia and cited by Ruth Towse in the edited volume, *A Textbook of Cultural Economics* (2019). It was believed that the criteria used by Throsby, including, for instance, the criterion of receiving remuneration for artistic work for the last five years, or of creating works according to the standards of creative work, would be adequate for research done in Poland. The 'professional' aspect of this definition excluded hobbyists and amateurs from the research. Ilczuk, Dudzik, Gruszka and Jeran made the definition more precise in the 2013 research project through screening, i.e. determining all additional criteria. Thresholds were also determined, which helped to specify the object of research provided in the definition above. It was assumed that a professional artist is a person whose 50% of revenue in the year gone by (30% in the case of literary artists), as against overall revenue, had been derived from artistic work. In addition, artists had to meet at least one of the following requirements that refer to the quality of their work:

- having received an award for artistic work
- taking part in exhibitions/concerts/vernissages, being an individual who is recognised in the artistic community
- being a member of an association of artists or creators.

This way of defining a professional artist was consequently used in the series of research conducted by Ilczuk. Only once, during the research on theatre artists during the COVID-19 pandemic, were the thresholds changed. In the course of the research, this level proved to be too exclusive. Opinions from organisations and firms within the industry, as well as from the survey participants, were taken into consideration and the approach was verified negatively. In the research on the professional group size, all individuals reported by organisations within the industry were considered along with individuals self-reporting their professional commitment as artists, creators or performers.

The second approach to defining the concept, which was different, was used in estimating the number of professionally active representatives of this professional group in Poland. A conscious decision was made not to define the terms 'artist' and 'creator,' since the meanings are not very precise and the terms usually generate superfluous discussions. In line with the accepted operational definition, the object of the population size research included individuals performing the artistic work professionally. Naturally, it should be highlighted that what was meant was only the work of individuals who were professionally active in performing artistic work, as opposed to office, organisational or technical work. Identifiers were those professions practised by specific individuals. The research included the following industries, which were indicated by the commissioner of the research project: film, literature, music, visual arts, dance, theatre and folk art. For each of these industries, the commissioner prepared a catalogue of professions that create the industry itself. The basis for preparing the list of professions was a series of open debates, organised within the National Conference of Culture, which is discussed in more detail in Chapter 5. The assumption adopted in the previous studies was consistently maintained, i.e. individuals living from creative or artistic activity, for whom this activity is an essential component of their household budget, would be counted.

## 1.4 Monitoring and analysing the labour market of artists

The basic indicators used to describe the labour market were formulated by the International Labour Office (ILO) in 1999, and have been used to prepare macroeconomic analyses, allowing for international comparison. For our microeconomic approach, we chose only some of these indicators, including working time, underemployment, part-time employment, unemployment, poverty, remuneration levels and 'the working poor.' The final indicator is connected with the concept of the precariat, which has attracted scholarly attention, most notably concerning the context of artists. Discussions about the precariat are dominated not so much by poverty as by insecurity in the labour market, insecurity of income or representation (cf. e.g. Standing 2004). When it comes to the other indicators, we can observe that in the context of rapid changes in the labour market the semantic dimension of the word 'unemployment' does not always have to mean a lack of work; instead, there may be a great work, but nobody is willing to pay for it (Boeri and van Ours 2021).

When embarked on our research, we asked ourselves the question, 'What do we know about the labour market of artists, based on existent research, reports and statistics?' The answer to this question is rather precursory: we know far too little. Indeed, the topic is often an object of interest on the part of the media; but apart from limited information taken from public statistical data, the scope of activities undertaken to monitor and analyse the professional situation of artists and creators is definitely too narrow when compared to other markets. However, the situation differs in terms of geography. An example of a model that would be difficult to achieve may be the method employed in France for monitoring and analysing the professional situation of artists overseen by the *Département des études, de la prospective et des statistiques – DEPS*) in the Ministry of Culture and Communication. Monitoring is also carried out regularly in Finland, the Netherlands, Germany, South Korea and Lithuania. Another good example is the joint action of public authorities and academia or a study led by Throsby, which is repeated every few years and provides an analysis of the condition and professional problems of artists in Australia.

Analyses of the labour market of artists are primarily aimed at recognising market institutions, identifying tendencies and problems of artists and creators of the labour market in terms of different professional industries, while taking into account both the supply side (artists and creators) and the demand side (representatives of institutions and enterprises employing artists and creators).

The main research problems may be defined as follows (Ilczuk et al. 2020):

- educational paths
- the professional path of graduates of arts schools
- the specifics and conditions of practising the profession by artists and creators, including the form of employment, areas of professional activity, sources of financing professional work of artists and creators, old-age pension system, etc.
- the economic situation of artists and creators in terms of professional groups, age and gender
- the scale and forms of public interventionism for the sake of artists and creators
- recommendations regarding the labour market of artists and creators (addressed to the main stakeholders of the research, such as public authorities, artistic communities or researchers) and regarding monitoring and analysing the professional labour market of artists and creators.

In Poland, state monitoring and analysis of the labour market of artists is at an early stage of development. The community of creative workers is dispersed, which has meant poor research outcomes. What is more, there are not even a modest number of studies; rather there are random and incidental projects undertaken in this area. Unfortunately, there are no connections between these studies, whether chronological or conceptual. We can forget about any comparisons. Reports and studies prepared within the industry by individual creative and artistic communities are also not suitable for comparative analyses. Their great value, topicality and high degree of representativeness should be emphasised; however, they usually provide pictures of only one professional group developed with various research methods. Public statistics in the case of artists and creators provide limited data. They are either concerned only with the graduates of art schools or result from research conducted on a group of entities employing at least ten employees, therefore they do not cover the smallest, but also potentially the most numerous business entities.

## References

Baumol, B., & Bowen, W. G. (1966). *Performing arts: The economic dilemma.* Cambridge: The MIT Press.

Begg, D., Fisher, S., & Dornbusch, R. (1993). Ekonomia, vol. 2. Państwowe Wydawnictwo Ekonomiczne, Warszawa.

Boeri, T., & van Ours, J. (2021). *The economics of imperfect labour markets.* Princeton: Princeton University Press

Bourdieu, P. (1986). The forms of capital. In John G. Richardson (Ed.), *Handbook of theory and research for the sociology of education* (pp. 241–258). New York: Greenwood.

Caves, R. E. (2000). *Creative industries: Contracts between art and commerce (No. 20).* Cambridge: Harvard University Press.

CICERONE Creative Industries Cultural Economy Production Network, Objectives. https://cicerone-project.eu/objectives/ (17.09.2023).

Coe, N. M. (2015). Global production networks in the creative industries. In: C. Jones, M. Lorenzen and J. Sapsed (Eds.) The Oxford Handbook of Creative Industries. Oxford: Oxford University Press: 486–501.

Dworzak, A. (2013). *Genialny twórca czy zmyślny przedsiębiorca? Studium z problematyki twórczości wielkich warsztatów artystycznych na Rusi Koronnej w XVIII wieku.* Wydawnictwo Uniwersytetu Jagiellońskiego. https://www.uj.edu.pl/documents/40768330/3f2e2438-a423-4bf1-9b39-9a08c393a2a1#page=134&view=Fit

Elberse, A. (2013). *Blockbusters: Why big hits–and big risks–are the future of the entertainment business.* London: Faber & Faber.

Garbicz, M., & Golachowski, E. (2012). Elementarne modele makroekonomiczne. Oficyna Wydawnicza Szkoły Głównej Handlowej, Warszawa.

Golka, M. (1991). Rynek sztuki. Agencja badawocz promocyjna Artia.

Hobday, M. (2000). The project-based organisation: An ideal form for managing complex products and systems? *Research Policy, 29,* 871–893.

Howkins, J. (2002). *The creative economy: How people make money from ideas.* UK: Penguin.

Ilczuk, D., Gruszka-Dobrzyńska, E., Socha, Z., & Hazanowicz, W. (2020). Policzone i policzeni! Artyści i artystki w Polsce, Wydawnictwo Uniwersytetu SWPS – Dom Wydawniczy Elipsa, Warszawa.

Ilczuk, D., & Karpińska, A. (2017). Kultura jako koło zamachowe rozwoju gospodarki [w:] C. Obracht-Prondzyński, P. Zbieranek (red.), Pomorskie poszerzenie pola kultury. Dylematy – konteksty – działania, Nadbałtyckie Centrum Kultury, Pomorskie Centrum Badań nad Kulturą UG, Gdańsk.

Ilczuk, D. (2012) Ekonomika kultury. PWN. Warszawa.

Ilczuk, D. (2013). *Rynek pracy artystów i twórców w Polsce*. Raport z badań, Bydgoszcz–Warszawa: Ministerstwo Kultury i Dziedictwa Narodowego.

Ilczuk, D., Dudzik, T., Gruszka, E., & Jeran, A. (2015). Artyści na rynku pracy. Wydawnictwo Attyka.

KEA European Affairs. (2006). The economy of culture in Europe. https://ec. europa.eu/assets/eac/culture/library/studies/cultural-economy_en.pdf

Nelson, R. H. (2015). *Economics as religion: From Samuelson to Chicago and beyond*. Philadelphia: Penn State Press.

Newbigin, J., Rosselló, P., & Wright, S. (2010). *The creative economy: An introductory guide*. London: British Council.

OECD. (2022). *The culture fix: Creative people, places and industries, local economic and employment development (LEED)*. Paris: OECD Publishing.

O'Hara, P. A. (2019). Mixed economy. In *The International Encyclopedia of Anthropology*. Wiley-Blackwell. Hoboken: Wiley-Blackwell.

Power, D., & Jansson, J. (2004). The emergence of a post-industrial music economy? Music and ICT synergies in Stockholm, Sweden. *Geoforum, 35*, 425–439.

Power, D., & Hallencreutz, D. (2002). Profiting from creativity? The music industry in Stockholm, Sweden and Kingston, Jamaica. *Environment and Planning A, 34*(10), 1833–1854.

Pratt, A. C. (2006). Advertising and creativity, a governance approach a case study of creative agencies in London. *Environment and Planning A, 38* (10), 1883–1899.

Rosen, S. (1981). The economics of superstars. *The American Economic Review, 71*(5), 845–858. http://www.jstor.org/stable/1803469

Samuelson, P. A., & Nordhaus, W. D. (2010). *Economics* (19th ed.). New York: McGraw-Hill.

Smith, A. (1937). The wealth of nations [1776] (Vol. 11937). na.

Standing, G. (2004). The Precariat. *Contexts, 13*(4), 10–12.

Szaban, J. (2013). Rynek pracy w Polsce i w Unii Europejskiej. Difin, Warszawa.

Throsby, D. (2001). *Economics and culture*. Cambridge: Cambridge University Press.

Throsby, D. (2008). The concentric circles model of the cultural industries. *Cultural Trends, 17*(3), 147–164.

Throsby, D. (2010). Ekonomia i kultura, tłum. O. Siara, Narodowe Centrum Kultury, Warszawa.

Towse, R. (2019). *A textbook of cultural economics*. Cambridge: Cambridge University Press.

UNCTAD. (2008). Creative Economy Report 2008: The Challenge of Assessing the Creative Economy: Towards Informed Policy-Making. United Nations, https://unctad.org/system/files/official-document/ditc20082cer_en.pdf

UNESCO. (2022). Re|Shaping policies for creativity. https://unesdoc.unesco.org/ark:/48223/pf0000380474

# 2 Public support for artists and creators in selected countries

## 2.1 Inspirations for a Polish model of support for artists and creators

Let us go a step further. Since in Poland we knew little about the professional situation of artists and creators; and additionally, there has been no great interest in bringing about change in this regard, it is not even surprising that there has been a dearth of proposed mechanisms. By contrast, we have a colourful palette of numerous solutions directly aimed at artists living in other countries.

*On the European map of the professional situation of artists, a multitude of solutions can be found in this area and, despite being aware of their limitations, it is worth reaching for them. The Nordic countries draw attention, where the level of access to social benefits is so high that there is no need to use solutions dedicated to artists, as, for example, in the countries of Central Europe.* (Ilczuk, Karpińska and Stano-Strzałkowska 2017, p. 1)

That is why in 2017, Dorota Ilczuk, together with Anna Karpińska and Sylwia Stano-Strzałkowska, prepared the expert report *Wsparcie dla twórców i artystów, perspektywa międzynarodowa* (Ilczuk, Karpińska and Stano-Strzałkowska 2017). The main aim of the report was to present the organisation of the artists' labour market in different countries and the factors influencing this organisation. As an extensive analysis of solutions and good practices, the report focused on public support provided by state and local authorities responsible for culture in selected countries. The starting point of choice was the European model of cultural policy, based on the significant involvement of the state and local authorities in the processes of designing and implementing cultural policy. The following European countries were selected for the analysis: Austria, the Czech Republic, Finland, France, Germany, Lithuania, the Netherlands and the United Kingdom. This list was supplemented by non-European countries, Australia, Brazil, Canada and South Korea.

Each of the presented country profiles had the same structure. The following aspects were analysed: the general conditions for practising

DOI: 10.4324/9781003401032-3

creative work, the status of the artist, the means used to monitor and analyse the cultural and creative sectors, remuneration, insurance and social security, the promotion of artists abroad, the organisation of the labour market for artists and creators, and the adaptation of education to its requirements.

It has been six years since the publication of the first report; and much has happened since then, including the COVID-19 pandemic, which affected the well-being of artists and creators. The extensive work put into updating all information has shown how flexible cultural policy needs to be, especially in emergencies. And so, we have chosen to present here only those solutions that we found interesting and inspiring; in particular for the newly created system of support for professional artists in Poland. That is why we have decided to divide this chapter following the new model of support for artists and creators proposed by Ilczuk, which is discussed in more detail in Chapter 6. We took into consideration:

1 Monitoring and analysis
2 Status of artists
3 Insurance and social security
4 Remuneration – influential factors
5 Promoting artists abroad
6 Organisation of the labour market and adaptation of education to its requirements

### 2.2   Monitoring and analysis

An important role in the support for artists is played by the monitoring and analysis of the socio-economic situation of this professional group. The authors of the *Wsparcie dla twórców i artystów, perspektywa międzynarodowa* (Ilczuk, Karpińska and Stano-Strzałkowska 2017) study drew particular attention to solutions from a non-European country, Australia.

The income situation of artists in Australia was well illustrated by the titles of two reports on this subject, which were published in 2010. Both were presented by the Australia Council for the Arts. The first, prepared by Throsby, is entitled *Do you Really Expect to Get Paid? An Economic Study of Professional Artists in Australia* (Throsby 2010); the second one, done by Cunningham, is entitled *What's your Other Job? A Census Analysis of Arts Employment in Australia* (Cunningham 2010). The vast majority of Australian artists are not able to make a living from artistic work alone. The debate over their pay has been going on for several decades but has not led to a systematic solution. Before the elections in 2010, there had been a specific project to create a Foundation for the Artist, which would involve state, private and corporate funds to support artists and their new artistic projects. These funds would, by definition, supplement (rather than replace) existing grant programmes or support programmes for artists and creative innovators in areas that have not been covered by such support. However, it was not possible to create such a foundation.

Research on the economic situation of artists has the longest tradition in Australia. Commissioned by the Australia Council for the Arts, the first analysis was carried out in 1981, and was conducted by a team of researchers from Macquarie University led by Professor David Throsby. Recognising the number of professional artists active in the country, their career paths and the revenues generated led to the establishment of a reasonable policy affecting this professional group. Moreover, it contributed to redefining the significance of arts and culture for the economy of Australia. The same team conducted subsequent surveys in 1983, 1987, 1993 and 2002. The 2002 survey showed, for example, that there were 45,000 artists, with the largest group being musicians and visual artists; and the smallest being dancers. The survey included eleven professional groups, i.e. writers, visual artists, artistic craftsmen, actors, directors, dancers, choreographers, musicians, singers, composers and cultural animators.

The term 'professionals,' when related to culture in Australia, apart from actors, dancers, musicians, visual artists, sculptors, architects, culture experts and animators, includes the following professions: journalists, web designers, producers, clowns, circus performers, hypnotists as well as religious leaders and clergy.

The monitoring and analysis of the cultural sector in Finland is carried out by several organisations, including, for instance, the Centre for Cultural Policy Research CUPORE, the National Audiovisual Institute and the Arts Promotion Centre Finland. Their work includes the question of the status of the artist and the labour market for artists. For instance, in 2001 the Arts Council of Finland commissioned a survey which followed the Australian method of researching artists developed by Throsby. The interpretation used in the survey assumed that artists are individuals belonging to associations and professional unions or benefitting from public grants given to creators (Ilczuk et al. 2015). In 2010, there was another survey done by the Arts Promotion Centre Finland, authored by Kaija Rensujeff and titled *The Status of the Artist in Finland – The Structure of the Artist Community*, *Work and Income Formation*. It followed the same methodology and definition of an artist, which guaranteed the continuity and comparability of both surveys.

## 2.3 Status of artists

From the point of view of creating a support system for creators, the status of an artist is used to define the freedoms and rights that the creator should be entitled to. Thanks to the efforts of UNESCO and the International Labor Organization, a resolution was adopted in Belgrade in 1980, which contained a number of recommendations regarding the working conditions of artists, the use of their labour rights and the need to introduce the institution of the 'social status of the artist' in legal systems.

From the point of view of the construction of the artist support system, defining who can have the status of an artist is a key issue. On this basis, it will be possible to grant special rights to artists. Eligibility criteria may vary, from membership in industry associations, through education, to income.

> *The practice in determining the status of artists is diverse and allows for both legal regulation of the status of the artist and granting the status by environmental organizations (unions and associations) and specially appointed commissions, usually located at public bodies and offices responsible for the sphere of culture.* (Ilczuk, Karpińska and Stano-Strzałkowska 2017, p. 78)

Interesting and extensive solutions regarding the status of artists can be found in Canada where the *Status of the Artist Act* was introduced in 1995. The act officially recognises the contribution of artists to the cultural, social and political life of Canada. It also specifies the professional status of the artist. It grants artists and producers the right to freedom of expression and association. Associations established by artists and producers receive the full right to represent their members in legal disputes and to strive for their socio-economic well-being. The *Status of the Artist Act* applies only to artists employed by the federal government. It does not apply to artists working on an employer-employee basis; nor does it apply to those commissioned within provincial structures. Canadian labour law is subject to the jurisdiction of a specific province, so it is different depending on the location. The first province to create its own legislation on the status of the artist was Quebec; however, after the *Status of the Artist Act* had been implemented, the other provinces started working on adequate legal regulations as well.

The *Status of the Artist Act* defines an artist, according to which a professional artist:

1 has to be an author of artistic, dramatic, literary or musical works within the meaning of the relevant copyright act; this group includes directors responsible for the overall direction of audiovisual works
2 has to perform, sing, recite, direct or act in a musical, literary or dramatic work, or in a circus, variety, mime or a puppet show
3 has to contribute to the creation of any production in the performing arts, music, dance, film, radio and television, video, sound-recording, dubbing, the recording of commercials, arts and crafts or the visual arts, and other disciplines that fall within the classification indicated in the relevant act.

The act specifies the meaning of the professional status in artistic work. In order to become a professional as stipulated by the legal regulations, a creator must meet at least one of the following criteria:

1 be paid for the work or presentation of the work before an audience and be recognised as an artist by other artists
2 be 'in the process of becoming an artist' in accordance with the practice of the artistic community
3 be a member of an artists' association (*Canadian Status of the Artist Act* 1992).

Solutions related to the introduction of the status of an artist were also introduced by Poland's neighbour – Lithuania where it has been legally regulated since 1996 by the power of the act *Republic of Lithuania Law on the Status of an Artist and the Status of an Organisation of Artists*, with later amendments from 2004 and 2010. According to the act (Article 2), an artist is 'a natural person who creates art works, performs them in a distinctive manner' (Act No I-1494). The status of a professional artist may be acquired by meeting one of seven conditions listed in the act (they are connected with education or the actual artistic work): the individual's works have been recognised as professional art in relevant monographs, reviews or articles written by experts in the field of the arts; the individual's works or artistic achievements are included in curricula of general education or arts education; the individual has received one of national awards in the field of the arts or an international award or a different local award within the relevant industry; the individual's works have been acquired by national museums or galleries in Lithuania or abroad; the individual holds a doctoral or a master's degree in the arts or has published an expert article or a critical article in the field of the arts in a Lithuanian or foreign artistic or scientific journal within the period of the last five years; the individual teaches or holds the position of a professor or a docent at a higher education institute, which offers education in the field of the arts according to the approved curricula; the individual has represented Lithuania (either individually or in a group) at international artistic events.

The status of a professional artist may be confirmed by either a registered association of art creators or a special body consisting of seven members appointed by the Ministry of Culture (the so-called Council for Granting the Status of an Artist). Granting the status of the artist has to be approved by the Minister of Culture. It is also possible to grant such a status by order of the Minister of Culture. The status of a professional artist may be lost (if the dissemination of the artworks done by the artist goes unnoticed, if the status of the artist was obtained illegally or if the court establishes the fact of artistic plagiarism). The loss of the status of the artist also has to be approved by the Minister of Culture. The Ministry of Culture keeps a digital register of professional artists (i.e. those that enjoy the relevant legal status) and of officially recognised organisations of artists. Each artist has a unique number in the database, referred to as the National Register of Artists.

According to the act mentioned above, artists who are considered professional may receive public grants and awards, have the right to bring their works of art created abroad to Lithuania in accordance with special rules, may be covered by the governmental Programme for Social Security of Artists (defined in a separate act), which guarantees benefits for artists receiving low or irregular income or artists who are in creative standstill (this applies to various cases, e.g. temporal problems of stage artists, i.e. dancers, musicians or singers, who cannot perform their roles on stage; or the difficulties of conceptual artists in realising their projects; the help is aimed at individuals in their working age who cannot work because of objective reasons).

### 2.4   Insurance and social security

In 2007, a resolution of the European Parliament recommended the creation of solutions dedicated to artists to provide them with a living basis. The creation of the recommendation and various activities resulted in a partial transformation of the legislation of some countries.

Many countries offer interesting solutions related to artists' insurance. In Germany, there is a system of old-age pension security, as well as social security support for artists, to include creators, performers and independent journalists. The system also encompasses invalidity insurance, and health and care insurance. Artists and journalists are obliged to cover half of the social security contribution. The amount, which in the case of an employment relationship would be paid by the employer, is to be paid by those business entities that purchase works of art and launch them in the market. Frequently, the costs of the employer are covered by subsidies of particular states. These regulations stem from the act on the compulsory social security of artists, which was introduced in 1981. In the case of individuals with permanent employment contracts, the rules on general insurance apply.

According to Article 1 of the act on the social security of artists, *Künstlersozialversicherungsgesetz* (1981) – *KSVG*, an artist means an individual practising the work of a musician, visual artist or performance artist or an individual teaching one of these professions. A publicist means an individual who works and creates as a writer or journalist or does other forms of activity similar to writing and journalism. Individuals who teach journalism are also insured under the *KSVG*. Artistic and journalistic work has to be performed by the individual covered by this insurance professionally and has to be the basis of a commercial activity.

In the Netherlands, the act *Wet Werk en Inkomen Kunstenaars* (*WWIK*) was an interesting solution in terms of social security for artists experiencing financial hardship. It gave artists the possibility of availing themselves of a temporary benefit amounting to 70% of the minimum wage. Artists could draw down these payments for 48 months within a longer period of 10 years. Due to a lack of income liquidity, artists could receive benefits in months when they did not have any revenue without having to use this support continuously. However, this act was repealed on January 1, 2012, since it was assumed that artists should develop their business acumen by selling their own products and reaching a wider group of recipients. The new policy was meant to encourage artists to earn their own living: it involved not only the repeal of the *WWIK* Act but also the limiting of subsidies. The entrepreneurship of artists is to be supported by foundations and institutions, whose aims are to organise events and bring artists into contact with other institutions, including international ones. Such undertakings would also anticipate the organisation of various types of lectures, debates and other educational activities.

A very extensive social security system can be observed in France where, the social security system for artists is based on two associations, i.e. *La Maison des Artistes (MDA)* aimed at visual artists, and *AGESSA – Association pour la Gestion de la Sécurité Sociale des Auteurs*, which brings together authors and creators, including literary artists and composers. Being granted membership in one of the associations is tantamount to recognising that a specific individual is a professional artist or creator, and this recognition is connected with various rights. The associations enable their members to pay social security contributions: *MDA,* only visual artists and *AGESSA,* other artists. They also keep registers of artists and creators as well as distributors of their works for the purpose of taxation. Creators who are freelancers, which in France is subject to different regulations, or who have their own businesses pay their contributions through the *RIS – Régime social des indépendants* system.

The social security system for artists is financed with their contributions as well as the contributions paid by individuals, companies and institutions that disseminate or use artists' works, i.e. by distributors. In 2019, a social security system for artists was established. Currently, to be covered by old-age pension security, it is necessary to have a revenue of EUR 1,505. Full social security (including sickness benefits, maternity allowances, invalidity pension and death benefits) covers artists who have earned at least 900 hours on a minimum wage, e.g. in 2019 it amounted to EUR 9,027. The right to be covered by social security in the following year is determined based on tax declarations. The amount of the contribution to be paid depends on the amount of the income earned. Artists who receive a yearly income which is lower than the level required to be covered by social security may voluntarily decide to pay a lump sum or pay contributions proportionate to their income, which, however, does not allow them to enjoy all social rights.

The so-called *Intermittents du spectacle* is a special solution aimed at stage artists (including, for instance, opera singers or orchestra conductors). Created in 1936 for the technical personnel in the film industry and extended in 1969 to include artists, the system is an answer to idle times in the work of performers. Since idle time is a part of the performing arts, which may lead to losing the right to social security, individuals covered by the solution are treated as full-time employees. It means that even during the period when they are unemployed, they still have the right to social security. They also receive an additional type of benefit for this period. In order to become a beneficiary of the system, an individual has to present proof of having worked at least 507 hours in the period of 304 days per year and having a monthly income that does not exceed the amount of EUR 4,500 (Karpińska 2021).

In Austria according to the federal act on supporting culture, i.e. *Kunstförderungsgesetz*, scholarships, awards and some public subsidies were exempted from income tax. This applied to, e.g. scholarships, awards and subsidies granted by the Austrian Film Institute (*Österreichisches Filminstitut*) for film concepts and scripts, revenue and financial help from public funds, or from public and private funds of various foundations.

For a long time, there was no specific solution that offered access to social benefits to artists working in all fields of the arts. Only musicians and visual artists were covered by a compulsory social security system. Other artists could individually obtain private insurance. Several funds were established to support artists in paying those optional social security contributions, e.g. *Künstlerhilfe-Fonds*.

The situation changed in 1997 with the adoption of an amendment to the act on employment and social security, which, among other things, stipulated that all freelancers now had to work under one of two types of contract: either the so-called *Werkvertrag*, i.e. a contract for work, aimed by definition at individuals without registered business activities, or the so-called *freier Dienstvertrag*, i.e. a contract of service, which by definition was aimed at self-employed individuals. The second type of contract included more social security benefits, but still far fewer than what a permanent employment contract would provide. According to the act, everyone (irrespective of the form of contract, i.e. *Werkvertrag* or *freier Dienstvertrag*) who within one tax year earns more than a specified amount of money has to obligatorily and individually pay social security contributions.

In South Korea, the difficult material situation of artists led to several cases of suicide in the 2000s that were widely discussed. The suicide of the film director Kwak Ji-kyoon in May 2010 was a particularly painful case. In his farewell letter, he wrote that he could not bear the pressure associated with the lack of work, and the absence of professional stability and clear prospects, to name just a few reasons. There was also the death of the young screenwriter Choi Go-eun, who died alone and in impoverished circumstances. These deaths both sparked a nationwide discussion about the material situation and social security needs of artists. This resulted in the passing of a special piece of legislation related to the social security of artists, known as the *Artist Welfare Act*, commonly referred to as the Choi Go-eun Act in honour of the deceased screenwriter. Passed in October 2011, this legislation came into effect in November 2012, with the establishment of the Korean Artists Welfare Foundation. The foundation has been operating officially since 22 January 2014, when it was granted a yearly budget of KRW seven million, which at the time equalled USD 6.4 million. The task of the foundation is to support artists who are experiencing financial difficulties (mainly due to a sudden decrease in income or an accident) and to provide them with some benefits as a form of temporary help throughout the period when they are looking for new commissions or have decided to change the profession. In addition, it is possible to take out insurance against professional risk *culture* (Ilczuk, Karpińska and Stano-Strzałkowska 2017).

### 2.5 Remuneration – influential factors

Research conducted around the world confirms that artists' salaries are very low. Only a very small group of stars achieve dizzying earnings. Usually, the profession of a creator and artist does not guarantee income at a level that ensures social security, so non-artistic work is a must.

*Therefore, the governments of many countries apply various types of solutions and mechanisms that have a direct impact on increasing the level of income earned by artists and offsetting the negative effects related to the specificity of artistic work. We also have such programs and mechanisms in Poland. However, their scale and scope are insufficient. The lack of detailed solutions concerning, for example, stimulating the demand for cultural goods and services is acute.* (Ilczuk, Karpińska and Stano-Strzałkowska 2017 p. 83)

An interesting way to stimulate demand was introduced in Brazil. Vale Cultura is a special pre-paid card promoted by the state and given to employees, onto which employers can load a monthly amount of BRL 50. The card can then be used for purchasing cultural goods (tickets, books or music). Apart from tangible goods, the programme allows participants to develop their skills, e.g. by signing up for dance classes. As is the case with transport or food allowances, the money loaded onto the employee's card is non-taxable (Cunha Filho 2022).

The programme cannot be joined by a natural person. However, artists belonging to associations or groups, who can sell their works in accordance with the conditions of the programme, may join. There is quite a long list of entities that operate in the area of culture that may register as providers of cultural goods and services. Currently, the information on Vale Cultura is available at the Ministry of Tourism of Brazil.

Another method of increasing demand was adopted in Finland where a regulation which stipulates that 1% of the costs of building public buildings goes to purchasing contemporary works of art was introduced. Such initiatives are meant to support the well-being of the arts.

An interesting phenomenon typical for the Czech Republic is a basic arts school, which offers a comprehensive programme of extra-curricular arts education pathways. In line with the national education programme, such schools offer education in the areas of music, dance, visual arts, literature and drama. Basic arts schools offer basic studies of the first and second levels, studies with an extended number of classes and adult education. The existence of such schools does not interfere with the existence of conservatories, which focus on developing the talents of students in the fields of music, theatre and dance. Conservatories prepare their students to work professionally in the field of arts and arts education. The high level of arts education has contributed to the increase in demand for the work of artists and creators. At the same time, schools are the places where a great many artists find permanent employment (Petrova).

Another way of influencing the level of remuneration of artists is the granting of grants and scholarships. In this case, the Polish model of supporting artists may be inspired by German solutions. All cultural institutions in Germany, both public and private, are supported by funds from the public purse. Contests for artists, awards given during such events and a well-developed system of scholarship play an important role as well.

On the federal level, support for artists is provided by organisations established for this purpose. These include the arts fund *Kunstfonds*, the literary fund *Deutscher Literaturfonds*, the socio-cultural fund *Fonds Soziokultur*, as well as the visual arts fund *Fonds Darstellende Künste*. There are also support funds from the German music council *Deutscher Musikrat*. The overall support includes scholarships, awards and other forms of support. Funding comes from federal funds as well as funds for promoting culture at the level of states. Scholarships and awards given to artists are an important instrument of support, which has been gaining even more importance over the years. It is almost impossible to indicate how many awards are currently issued in Germany: it is said that in 1998 there were about 2,000. A great many cities give their own awards as well, which may be exemplified by the Schwabing Art Prize awarded by Munich, the Cologne Fine Art Award, or the Goslarer Kaiserring Award given by the city of Goslar.

In addition, there is a well-developed system of support for artists in terms of help needed during exhibitions, while applying for grants, etc. The support for artistic productions in Germany includes, firstly, supporting artistic institutions, and secondly, creating creativity-friendly conditions. An important factor in financing culture is also sponsorship and patronage, as well as a well-developed base of the private sector, including corporate foundations working to support the arts. Another priority is support for individual creativity and creators from various industries. A special type of support is provided to freelancers and independent artists, which also covers undertakings and start-ups in the cultural and creative industries.

### 2.6  Promoting artists abroad

*Promoting and subsidizing artist mobility aims to support creators in reaching a wider audience, as well as enabling them to enter a larger market. The notion of mobility or foreign promotion of artists includes not only the possibility of exporting creativity, but also establishing contacts (networking), participation in artistic internships, tours and residencies.* (Ilczuk, Karpińska and Stano-Strzałkowska 2017, p. 95)

Many countries have programs supporting mobility addressed to artists and other employees in cultural and creative sectors. Their goal is to encourage not only the promotion of the culture of a given country but also the establishment of international cooperation and networking.

The government of Great Britain traditionally finances artistic activity according to 'the arm's length principle.' The government determines the general way of financing, but it is the special body called QUANGO that allocates the funds. Ministers enjoy some freedom in terms of distributing the funds, as they can have an influence on the structure of and changes within QUANGOs, impose limits of spending on administration or set goals and tasks, which QUANGOS have to achieve and complete. In the UK, there are four arts councils, i.e. Arts Council England, Arts Council of Northern Ireland, Arts Council of Wales, and Creative Scotland. Each of the four councils runs its own grant programme (Fisher, Figuera and Hadley).

The Artists' International Development Fund is a program co-funded by the British Council and Arts Council Northern Ireland. The program is developed to produce *a cadre of artists and creative practitioners in the UK (and also globally) who have experienced the benefits of international working between the UK and other countries and are advocates for it among their peers.* The second goal is

> *an increase in the amount of international collaboration among artists between the UK and other countries across the arts and creative industries* and *artistic development for artists. The programme supports early-stage international development opportunities for individual, freelance and*

*self-employed artists and organisations based in Northern Ireland. It will afford recipients the opportunity to spend time building links with artists, organisations and/or creative producers in another country.* (Artists' International Development Fund)

### 2.7 Organisation of the labour market and adaptation of education to its requirements

*Good organization of the labor market translates directly into the quality of working conditions for artists. Trade unions and trade unions fight for the rights of their members by negotiating collective labor agreements, lobbying for the benefit of the represented group and supporting associated artists in various activities. The level of professionalization of the market is also expressed in the well-established position of intermediary institutions (employment agencies, managers), which are a kind of link between creativity and the market.. Regardless of this, it is worth equipping future graduates of art schools with basic market competences. Adapting artistic education to market requirements helps young artists to start work, run their own business or cooperate with business. The possibility of additional training in the field of entrepreneurship in culture is also important.* (Ilczuk, Karpińska and Stano-Strzałkowska 2017, pp. 96–97)

In the Netherlands, there are a great many collective labour agreements (the so-called *collective arbeidsovereenkomst* or *CAO*), especially in the field of stage/theatre and other performing arts, but also more broadly in the cultural sector. Collective labour agreements are signed between the employer and employees, which means that they are binding only within one employment relationship. Most frequently, CAOs are used in the following fields: architecture, arts education, the media (journalism, publishers), museums and other types of exhibition activities, performance (dance, orchestra, theatre), public libraries and retail trade in musical instruments and scores. Employees of almost all fields of artistic and cultural activity are members of a federation of culture, i.e. *Federatie Cultuur*. This is an organisation which monitors negotiations of collective labour agreements, which take place every year between Dutch trade unions, organisations of employees and the central government (Brom).

The important role of the association of creators is played differently in Canada. Artists' associations, which often function as trade unions, are very important in the market. They represent self-employed artists associated with them to various institutions. They often fight over collective bargaining agreements that determine the salaries that artists receive. These types of institutions are supervised by the Canadian Artists and Producers Professional Relations Tribunal responsible for certifying these associations, but also for supervising and concluding collective agreements. The possibility of associating and creating strong unions for artists and producers is provided by the 1995 Status of Artist Act.

In Great Britain, the difficult situation of artists, long working hours, no leave, and considerable pressure, have all led to a situation in which problems with mental health are being observed among employees of the cultural and creative sectors more and more frequently. Because of this, the UK National Arts Wellbeing Collective was established. This is a network of exchanging experiences and best practices:

The purpose of the UK National Arts Wellbeing Collective ('UK NAWC') is to bring together Arts, Cultural and Heritage organisations, individuals and other interested parties to:

- share ideas on reducing the stigma of mental health in the workplace;
- identify trends and common challenges;
- discuss best practices to support mental health issues across the sector;
- promote good health and wellbeing within the sector
- provide a central database of members and useful wellbeing contacts.
(*UK National Arts Wellbeing Collective*)

The Vilnius Academy of Fine Arts (Lithuania) introduced the interesting educational imitative by launching in 2006,

> with the support from the European structural funds, the Design Innovation Center, which promotes cooperation between university students and business, including foreign ones. The Academy also established its subdivision in the city of Neringa (Nida) on the Curonian Spit – the Art Colony Nida (NAC) was opened in March 2011 thanks to the support of funds from the European Economic Area and the Norwegian Funds. NAC is a meeting place for artists, designers, architects, curators, art critics and researchers from around the world. NAC also runs an artist-in-residence program. (Ilczuk, Karpińska and Stano-Strzałkowska 2017, p. 99)

### 2.8   The international spectrum of support solutions for artists

It should be borne in mind that actions such as periodic monitoring and analysing the situation of artists and creators have had an invaluable impact in terms of creating solutions that may be tailored to a given situation. The method of monitoring and analysing the professional situation of artists in France has been very effective, with the Ministry of Culture cyclically investigating the problem. The analysis of good practice of a regular collection of data as one of the bases for enforcing cultural policy reveals even more the insufficient efforts that are made in this context in Poland; thus proving the validity of the hypothesis we put forward.

Promoting and subsidising the mobility of artists is also vital, as the aim of such actions would be to support artists in reaching a wider audience and facilitating their access to a larger market. The notion of mobility or the international promotion of artists includes the possibility of not only exporting creativity, but also establishing contacts (networking) and participating in artistic apprenticeships, tours or creative residencies. Supporting intercultural dialogue by way of cultural, intellectual and social exchange is one of the main goals of UNESCO (UNESCO 2005). In 2007, Poland ratified the UNESCO *Convention on the Protection and Promotion of the Diversity of Cultural Expressions of 20 October 2005.* One of the main principles included in the convention is the Rule of Solidarity and International Cooperation. In accordance with the Convention, the goal of the UNESCO World Observatory on the Social Status of the Artist is to collect data on supporting the mobility of artists in various countries.

Organisational measures and professionalisation of the labour market have led to amelioration in terms of the structures and instruments supporting creative work, which corresponds with the hypothesis concerning the mutual influence of cultural policy on the labour market of artists and sectors of the creative economy. Trade unions and associations within the industries have been traditionally fighting for the rights of their members: negotiating collective labour agreements, lobbying for the benefit of their represented groups, and supporting associated artists in various activities. The level of the professionalisation of the market is today visible through the well-established position of intermediary institutions (work agencies, managers) that act as a link between creativity and the market. A manager or an agent with adequate education and training should know legal regulations, and market rules, and, above all, should be able to support the artist in their administrative tasks, such as applying for a grant. Irrespective of these issues, it is worth equipping future graduates of art schools with basic market competencies. Adapting arts education to market requirements will underpin future projects, and give young creators the know-how needed to run their own companies and succeed in the business world. Additional training in the area of entrepreneurship in culture would also prove advantageous.

The situation of artists in the labour market is very complicated and this is a problem resulting from the specificity of artistic creation. In this sense, it is not a problem of a specific country, but a broader issue that is also receiving attention from UNESCO and the EU, which resulted in the issuance of recommendations regarding the status of the artist by these organizations. In this sense, national solutions for supporting artists do not arise in a vacuum, but they differ greatly from each other. This diversity results from different legislative systems and cultural policies. By taking a closer look at support models and recognizing their specificity, a map of good and interesting practices can be created. It can serve as an inspiration and guide in creating new solutions for artists.

### References

Brom, R. The Netherlands profile at compendium of cultural policies and trends in Europe. https://www.culturalpolicies.net/database/search-by-country/country-profile/?id=28

Canadian Status of the Artist Act. (1992). https://laws-lois.justice.gc.ca/eng/acts/S-19.6/

Cunha Filho, F. H. (2022). Plano Nacional de Cultura: análise jurídica da concepção, tramitação e potencialidades. *Educação E Pesquisa*, *48*, e244555. https://www.ris.bka.gv.at/GeltendeFassung.wxe?Abfrage=Bundesnormen&Gesetzesnummer=20001060, dostęp luty 2017

Cunningham, S. (2010). What's your other job? A census analysis of arts employment in Australia. *Australian Council for the Arts.*

Fisher, R., Figuera, C., & Hadley, S. The United Kingdom profile at compendium of cultural policies and trends in Europe. https://www.culturalpolicies.net/database/search-by-country/country-profile/?id=42

Ilczuk, D., Dudzik, T., Gruszka, E., & Jeran,A. (2015). Artyści na rynku pracy. Wydawnictwo Attyka, Kraków.

Ilczuk, D., Karpińska, A., & Stano-Strzałkowska,S. (2017). Wsparcie dla twórców i artystów. Perspektywa Międzynarodowa. https://nck.pl/upload/attachments/319282/Wsparcie%20dla%20twórców%20i%20artystów.%20Perspektywa%20międzynarodowa.pdf

Karpińska, A. (2021). Jak to działa w innych krajach? Ubezpieczenia społeczne artystów. Ruch Muzyczny 11/2021. https://ruchmuzyczny.pl/article/1150

Künstlersozialversicherungsgesetz, BGBl. I S. 705 (1981).

Petrova, P. The Czech Republic profile at compendium of cultural policies and trends in Europe. https://www.culturalpolicies.net/database/search-by-country/country-profile/?id=9

Rensujeff, K. (2003). The Status of the Artist in Finland – Report on Employment and Income Formation in Different Fields of Art. Arts Council of Finland, Helsinki.

Rensujeff, K. (2015). The status of the artist in Finland 2010 – The structure of the artist community, work and income formation. *Arts Promotion Centre Finland.*

Republic of Lithuania Law on the Status of an Artist and the Status of an Organisation of Artists, Act No I-1494 (1996).

Throsby, D. (2010). Do you really expect to get paid? An economic study of professional artists in Australia. *Australian Council for the Arts.*

UK National Arts Wellbeing Collective, Aims. https://www.abtt.org.uk/wp-content/uploads/2019/10/NAWC-Collective-Strategy.pdf

UNESCO. (2005). Convention on the protection and promotion of the diversity of cultural expressions. https://en.unesco.org/creativity/convention/texts.

# 3 The socio-economic situation of artists and creators in Poland

## Warsaw-Bydgoszcz study (2013)

### 3.1 Socio-economic situation of artists and creators

This chapter discusses the survey which gave rise to the research series that was done in 2013 by researchers from Warsaw and Bydgoszcz under the supervision of Professor Ilczuk. In the following chapters – Chapter 4 and Chapter 5, we develop the issue raised in 2013 during this first analytical project. In Chapter 4, we discuss the national survey for artists and creators, and in Chapter 5 we touch upon the issue of inequalities between women and men across artistic professions. Moreover, the second part of Chapter 5 is devoted to the unusual situation of theatre artists during the COVID-19 pandemic in Poland. These findings, along with the whole research series, allowed us to present in the course of the book, a holistic overview of the specifics of the work of artists and creators in the period between 2013 and 2019. It should be noted, though, that different methodologies that were used do not assume the carrying out of longitudinal studies and, because of this, the results of particular research components obtained over the years cannot be clearly compared. But let us begin in the year 2013.

One of the first parts of the research into the situation of artists in the labour market in Poland was done in the metropolitan area of the city of Warsaw, as well as the Bydgoszcz-Toruń metropolitan area in 2013. The results obtained in the course of the research demonstrated the problems and challenges within this specific professional group. Moreover, in the process of the research, the focus group interview (FGI) had been conducted. It was carried out with the supply side of the artistic labour market – the creators' employers.

It is worth noting that the research was done ten years ago; and so in this chapter, we present general tendencies and numbers connected with the specifics of artistic work, underlining that the survey from 2018 as well as the Warsaw part of the Warsaw-Bydgoszcz survey were both fully representative. Furthermore, it should be also highlighted that the research confirmed the hypothesis about the insufficient and unsystematic

DOI: 10.4324/9781003401032-4

process of monitoring and analysing the situation of artists in Poland. It is important that this statement led to another series of research led by Ilczuk.

The Warsaw-Bydgoszcz research project was implemented by the Pro Cultura Foundation in collaboration with the University of Economy in Bydgoszcz. It was co-financed by the Polish Ministry of Culture and National Heritage. It was carried out to identify trends and problems in the labour market of artists and creators in terms of sectors of activity, considering both the supply side and the demand side. This was the first study on the labour market of artists and creators covering more than one professional group after 1989, when the planned economy and one-party system were replaced by a market economy and democracy.

The research project was divided into three stages. During the first stage, desk research analysis was performed, including national and international data, regulations and press materials scientific assessment was made based on studies conducted abroad, Polish and international statistical data, regulations as well as press materials. During the second stage, field studies were done in the metropolitan area of Warsaw and the Bydgoszcz-Toruń metropolitan area including both quantitative and qualitative research (focus groups and individual interviews). The third and final stage was devoted to an analysis of the results of the secondary data research and the outcomes of the field studies.

During this process, several main research problems were addressed and analysed. They included the educational system path, professional career path of artists and creators, their economic situation, motivation for work or the specifics and conditions of practising the profession by artists and creators, as well as the problem of unemployment. What is more, the investigation included not only the perspective of artists and creators, but also the perspective of employers, which will be displayed in the section 3.1.5 of this chapter. These research problems, although indicative of past tendencies, which, however, are often valid and recurrent, are discussed below. What is more, this study gave a base to formulate further empirical questions in the next research projects.

### 3.1.1 Educational path

In the preliminary stage of the research, the following two assumptions have been made: firstly, it was agreed that arts education is a factor stimulating the professional success of artists; and secondly, that the internationalisation of education increases artists' chances in the labour market.

However, the results were quite surprising. Only 11% of the respondents said that they had completed art school at a secondary level, and

29.9% admitted that they had graduated from art school at the level of higher education. The greatest proportion of individuals possessing advanced education, amounting to 40%, was observed among those with the lengthiest tenure in the workforce, namely those born between 1930 and 1950. Conversely, within the most populous age cohort, born between 1971 and 1990, this percentage diminished to 20.6% (Ilczuk et al. 2013). It is noteworthy that this latter group exhibited the highest incidence of individuals who reported having attained secondary-level education in art schools. Substantial disparities in educational attainment across distinct professional cohorts were discernible, as exemplified in Figure 3.1.

As depicted in the figure, musicians exhibited the highest prevalence of having completed higher education in art disciplines, with 59.4% of individuals within the music profession falling into this category. Conversely, literary artists had the lowest proportion of graduates from higher-level art schools, constituting a mere 3.3%.

It is noteworthy to emphasize that the period spent in higher education not only facilitates the acquisition of specialized skills but also fosters the development of robust social networks. Such networks can play a pivotal role in advancing one's career prospects and creating barriers for potential competitors, a phenomenon substantiated by qualitative research findings.

In terms of post-diploma studies, musicians predominantly pursued further education in the arts, dancers gravitated towards pedagogy, and literary artists were more inclined towards management-related studies.

Following, having accepted the assumption that the internationalisation of education increases opportunities in the labour market, during the quantitative research, it was decided to investigate the degree of the internationalisation of education of the respondents and the level of participation in contests organised abroad, as well as the level of their activity aimed at obtaining grants offered abroad.

At the time of the study, the findings reflected a limited degree of internationalisation in education within the sample. Specifically, only one respondent had attained higher education qualifications abroad, and a minority of participants reported having pursued post-diploma studies abroad (5.5%). Similarly, a small fraction of respondents (4.7%) identified foreign grants as a notable source of financial support for their artistic endeavours. Furthermore, the percentage of individuals who claimed to have received awards in international competitions was also modest, standing at 4% (Ilczuk et al. 2013). It is plausible to assume that trends in this regard may have developed over the years. Nevertheless, a comprehensive investigation of this evolving trend remains imperative but has not been explored yet.

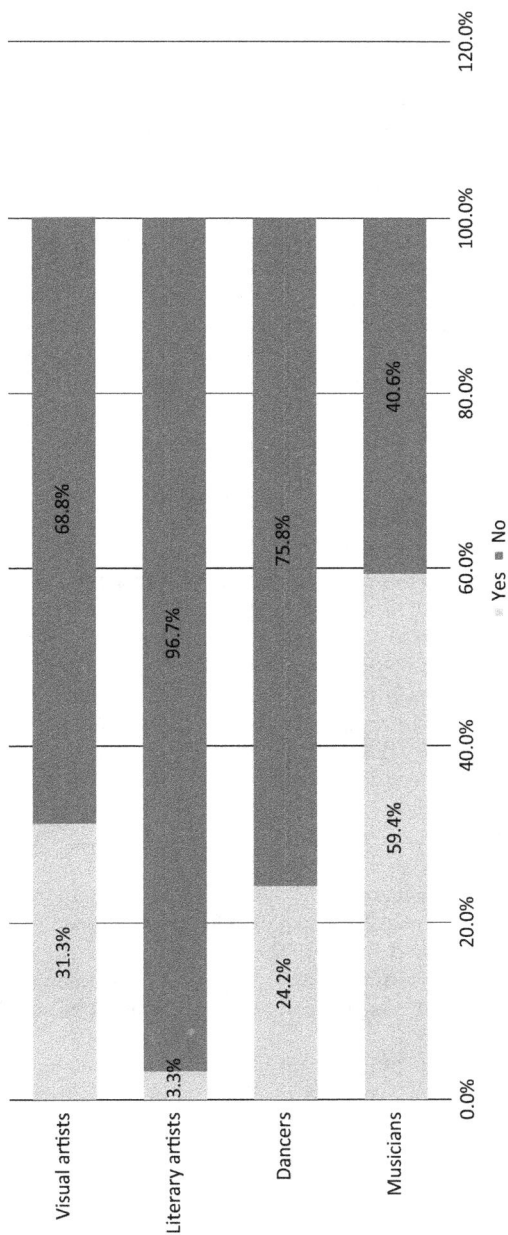

*Figure 3.1* Did you complete art school at the level of higher education?

*Source:* own work based on Indykator 2013.

### 3.1.2  *Professional career path of artists and creators*

In the effort to pinpoint the challenges artists faced then in the labour market, the prevailing belief was validated – that artists must collaborate with multiple organizations and excel in various roles. Moreover, there was a question raised about whether artists find employment outside cultural institutions – inside and outside the creative sector.

As demonstrated in the results, in 2013 the majority of respondents, just over 60%, exclusively practised a single artistic profession, which they identified as their 'main' and 'only' occupation. Among the various professional groups, literary artists were the most inclined to pursue only one profession (80%), while dancers showed the lowest tendency for such singularity (42%). Additionally, when considering collaborations with artistic institutions, 32.3% of respondents did not engage with any institutions, 20.5% partnered with a single institution, and 27.6% worked with more than four institutions. It's noteworthy that musicians and visual artists had the highest levels of engagement with multiple institutions (Ilczuk et al. 2013), as illustrated in Figure 3.2.

Inquiries regarding artists' engagements beyond the cultural realm considered two possibilities: artistic work and other forms of activity. Almost half of the respondents (47%) indicated employment in institutions outside the cultural domain. Predominantly, this entailed roles in the service industry, with 71.7% of respondents specifying functions unrelated to administration, local government or education. Interestingly, all female respondents, regardless of their profession, and 64.2% of male respondents (with visual artists being the most prevalent in this category) primarily reported engagements with entities outside the cultural sector (Ilczuk et al. 2013).

Among respondents engaged in artistic activities beyond the cultural sphere, a majority of collaborations were initiated by external entities. Specifically, the production department commenced these collaborations in 40% of instances, with men being more frequently approached in such scenarios. The management board instigated collaborations in 25.5% of cases, and the marketing department played a role in 18% of cases. When artists initiated such collaborations, it was more common among men, particularly visual artists, as opposed to women. Dancers were the sole exception in this group, where only females initiated such engagements.

It follows, then, that artists, except for literary artists, could devote their time mainly to artistic work (Ilczuk et al. 2013). However, they (i.e. those who answered the question) comprised only 54% of the survey sample.

The question of the time devoted to artistic work corresponded with the one about multiple professions, or multi-professionalism. The topic is discussed in more detail in the subsequent part of this book, considering

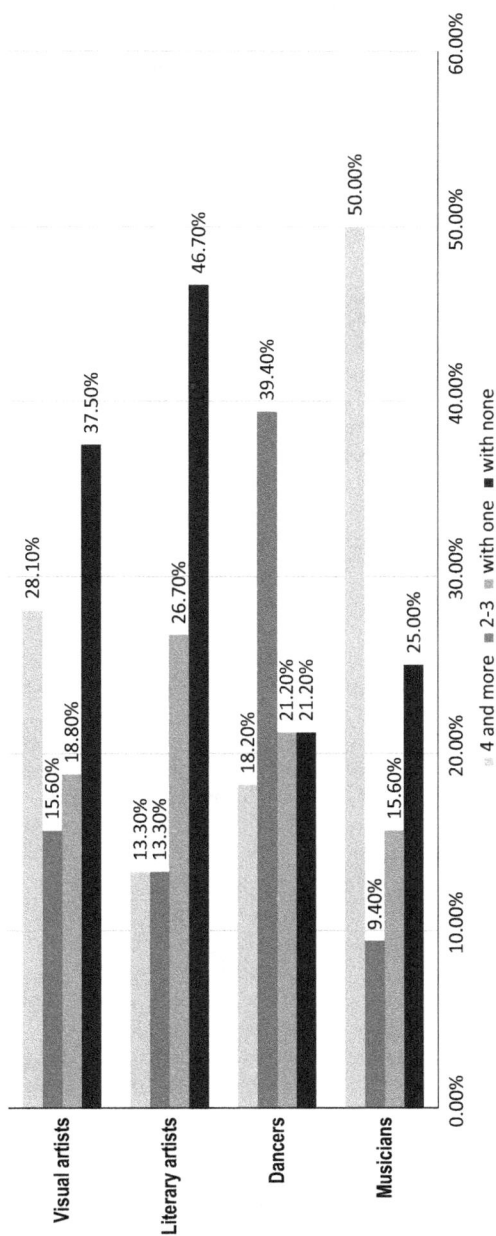

*Figure 3.2* With how many artistic institutions are you currently cooperating (including various legal forms of cooperation)?

*Source:* own work based on Indykator 2013.

the situation covering a later period – the year 2018. Nevertheless, in 2013 more than half of the respondents (53.6%), when asked about the amount of time they devoted to artistic work during the week, indicated the answer 'adequate,' while 29.3% would like to work more. 17.3% of the respondents claimed it was too much, with men providing this answer much more frequently than women. The answers to the question about the time that artists spend on artistic work across the professional groups are presented in Table 3.1. What is interesting, as indicated in the table, musicians most often complained about spending 'too little' time on artistic work, whereas dancers would spend 'too much' time.

When talking about the number of working hours spent on artistic work, most frequently, the respondents would indicate 40 hours per week (23%), but more than half of them (53%) reported a working week longer than the one indicated in the Labour Code. As proven by the research, in the year 2013 10.2% of the respondents worked from 60 to 70 hours per week. Female musicians and male literary artists proved to be the busiest group, which corresponds to their answers about time devoted to artistic work (Ilczuk et al. 2013).

The presented results indicate that the artists participating in the 2013 survey cooperated with a number of organisations, becoming self-fulfilled as artists. Approximately half of the respondents collaborated with organisations affiliated with the business sector. However, it is challenging to conclusively determine if these organisations specifically represented the creative industries. Nevertheless, the substantial number of respondents affirming their engagement in artistic work for employers outside the cultural realm suggests that this possibility is highly plausible.

We also took the opportunity to gauge participants' perceptions of their bargaining position in dealings with employers. We examined the validity of the notion that employers within the business industry hold a more favourable view of artists as employees compared to employers within the public cultural sector.

A strong and very strong negotiating position towards employers of the public cultural sector was reported by 41% of the respondents, with female dancers and male musicians being the most numerous groups. A weak and very weak position was reported by 26% of the respondents, who were most frequently the oldest of the respondents in the groups of female musicians and male dancers (Ilczuk et al. 2013).

Among almost half of the respondents who reported working outside the public cultural sector, 53.3% of the respondents (most frequently by male dancers and slightly less so by musicians, both females and males, and female visual artists) said they were in a strong and a very strong negotiating position. A weak and very weak position was reported by 15.3% of the respondents (most frequently by female and male literary artists and male musicians).

*Table 3.1* How do you assess the amount of time spent on artistic work over the last five years (across various professional groups)? N = 127

| | Too little Number of answers (N) | Percentage (%) | Adequate Number of answers (N) | Percentage (%) | Too much Number of answers (N) | Percentage (%) | Total Number of answers (N) | Percentage (%) |
|---|---|---|---|---|---|---|---|---|
| Musicians | 12 | 37.5 | 15 | 46.9 | 5 | 15.6 | 32 | 100 |
| Dancers | 7 | 21.2 | 17 | 51.5 | 9 | 27.3 | 33 | 100 |
| Literary artists | 10 | 33.3 | 17 | 56.7 | 3 | 10 | 30 | 100 |
| Visual artists | 8 | 25 | 19 | 59.4 | 5 | 15.6 | 32 | 100 |
| Total | 37 | 29.1 | 68 | 53.5 | 22 | 17.3 | 127 | 100 |

*Source:* Indykator 2013.

The findings regarding the acceptance and execution of work for cultural institutions led to a preliminary inference. It suggests the presence of signs indicating what is often referred to as 'cross-industrial mobility' in the labour market, a phenomenon further elaborated upon in Begg, Fisher and Dornbusch (1993, p. 316). This phenomenon has already signified a gradual rise in the availability of employment opportunities for artists beyond the confines of the cultural sector, which was proven in the later works by Ilczuk (2020).

### 3.1.3   Economic situation and work motivation

The results obtained in 2013 created the image of an artist who can, to a great extent, devote time to artistic work. The question about performing work which is not connected with the artistic profession outside the cultural sector was answered affirmatively by a relatively small group of the respondents (17.6%), with as many as 50% of them refusing to answer the question. Bearing in mind that half of the respondents perform artistic work for the sake of entities outside the sphere of culture, there was another issue raised – about the level of revenue earned from artistic activities and the motivation for performing work not connected with the profession in institutions outside the cultural sphere.

Despite the pessimistic picture evident in Table 3.2, in 2013 (what will change in the pandemic times, what we describe in Chapter 4.2) only 7.9% of the respondents considered resigning from the profession of an artist, most frequently providing the answer 'I do not know' to the question about a possible future profession (40% of the respondents among those 'considering changing the profession').

The professions of a manager and a teacher were indicated as alternatives with the same frequency (20% in each case). One individual from the oldest group of respondents indicated retirement as an alternative.

It should be recalled that only 14.7% of the female respondents and 20% of the male respondents said in 2013 that they performed work not related to the artistic profession in institutions outside the cultural sphere. Unfortunately, we did not ask a similar question about such activity in the cultural sphere (we only know that 20% of the respondents said they held a managerial position); however, based on a slightly larger group of the respondents who answered the question about the motivation for non-artistic work, it may be concluded that work not related to the artistic profession was performed also in cultural institutions. The most frequently indicated source of motivation for performing non-artistic work was a willingness to obtain funds for artistic activity (52% of the respondents, with women indicating it more frequently than

*Table 3.2* Information about the level of revenue in the survey sample. N = 127

|  | Number of answers (N) | Percentage (%) |
|---|---|---|
| Below PLN 20,000 (EUR 4,694) | 36 | 28.3 |
| PLN 20,000–30,000 (EUR 4,694–7,042) | 6 | 4.7 |
| PLN 30,001–40,000 (EUR 7,042–9,389) | 6 | 4.7 |
| PLN 40,001–50,000 (EUR 9,389–11,737) | 11 | 8.7 |
| PLN 60,001–70,000 (EUR 14,084–16,431) | 5 | 3.9 |
| PLN 70,001–80,000 (EUR 16,431–18,779) | 1 | 0.8 |
| PLN 80,001–90,000 (EUR 18,779–21,126) | 1 | 0.8 |
| Above PLN 100,000 (EUR 23,474) | 3 | 2.4 |
| No answer | 28 | 22.0 |
| 'I do not know' | 30 | 23.6 |
| Total | 127 | 100 |

*Source:* Indykator 2013.

men at the level of 64% and 47.7%, respectively). Other motivations were indicated less frequently (39%) and included, firstly, no possibility of securing a basic living standard from artistic work (with female musicians and male dancers being the largest group), secondly, willingness to ensure social security (with female musicians and male visual artists being the largest group) (Ilczuk et al. 2020).

A detailed analysis of each professional group is presented in Table 3.3.

Considering that only 67% of the respondents answered the question about the motivation for performing non-artistic work, the picture of the material situation of an artist does not seem to be very bad; however, the fact that for slightly more than 20% of the whole population of the artists participating in the survey, and particularly, for more than half of the visual artists who were questioned, it is not possible to achieve a basic living standard is of legitimate concern.

### 3.1.4   *The unique aspects and work environment of artists and creators*

The results obtained by investigating the motivations for undertaking work outside the cultural sphere justify the necessity to look into the answers to the question of whether the inability to secure health insurance and old-age pension security (both listed as significant motivations for undertaking work outside the artistic profession) are key risk factors when it comes to practising the profession of an artist and creator.

As demonstrated by the results, running a business was reported by 28.3% of the respondents, with 25.1% having a registered business (most frequently male visual artists) and 3.2% operating within

*Table 3.3* Basic motivations for performing non-artistic work across the professional groups. N = 127

| | Musicians Number of answers (N) | Percentage (%) | Dancers Number of answers (N) | Percentage (%) | Literary artists Number of answers (N) | Percentage (%) | Visual artists Number of answers (N) | Percentage (%) |
|---|---|---|---|---|---|---|---|---|
| The possibility of obtaining funds for artistic activity | 7 | 36.8 | 9 | 45.0 | 6 | 40.0 | 10 | 31.3 |
| No possibility of securing a basic living standard from artistic work | 4 | 21.0 | 4 | 20.0 | 3 | 20.0 | 12 | 37.5 |
| Ensuring social security | 5 | 26.3 | 5 | 25.0 | 4 | 26.7 | 9 | 28.1 |
| Self-fulfilment/ self-promotion | 2 | 10.5 | 1 | 0.5 | 1 | 3.3 | 0 | 0.0 |
| Helping others | 1 | 0.1 | 0 | 0.0 | 0 | 0.0 | 1 | 3.1 |
| Establishing new contacts | 0 | 0.0 | 1 | 0.3 | 1 | 9.1 | 0 | 0.0 |
| Total | 19 | | 20 | | 15 | | 32 | |

*Source:* Indykator 2013.

foundations (also most frequently visual artists, but this time including female artists).

Employment based on an employment contract was reported by 25.9% of the respondents (with 16.5% working for a non-definite period, most often male dancers, and 9.4% for a definite period, most often female musicians).

In the case of civil law contracts, the most frequently used form of employment in 2013 was a contract for work, reported by 52% of the respondents (most often musicians, and women rather than men). A contract of service was indicated by 23.5% of the respondents (most often both genders of visual artists and male musicians). The respondents did not expect any relevant changes in terms of formal aspects of the form of employment at any time over the next five years.

Considering the fact that only 16.5% of the respondents said they had an employment contract for a non-definite period, it may be stated that the level of insecurity in the labour market of the analysed group of artists was and is high (as the 2018 research will show).

The question about other forms of financing artistic work (grants, awards given in contests, sponsorship, patronage) was also a question about the demand for the work of artists generated by national institutions, institutions run by local authorities and companies outside the cultural sector.

Awards given in contests were the most frequently indicated source of funds (mainly national contests, reported by 18% of the respondents representing visual artists, mainly women). Second in terms of frequency were sponsorship and grants (mainly national). Grants were indicated most often by literary artists (men), whereas sponsorship was indicated by women. As many as 67% of the respondents did not indicate any of the options listed above as an additional source of revenue.

As many as 25.2% of the respondents reported that in the years 2008–2013, there had been times when the respondent had not been covered by health insurance and social security (most frequently male dancers and male literary artists).

Moreover, 23.1% of the respondents reported no health insurance in the last five years. Those were slightly more men than women, most often born between 1971 and 1990. Table 3.4 presents more detailed data.

Unemployment within the artistic community engenders distinct sentiments within the framework of financial stability, or more aptly expressed, the absence of financial gain, a predicament that has incited a wave of protests among artists and creators, not limited to Poland alone.

Within the scrutinized cohort of artists, 8.9% acknowledged their registration as unemployed within the preceding five years. This subset

*Table 3.4* Have there been any moments in time in the last five years of
performing artistic work when you were not insured? A lack of health
insurance across the professional groups and age groups of the
respondents. N = 127

|  |  | Yes Number of answers (N) | Percentage (%) | No Number of answers (N) | Percentage (%) |
|---|---|---|---|---|---|
| Musicians | 1930–1950 | 1 | 25.0 | 3 | 75.0 |
| Dancers |  | 0 | 0.0 | 0 | 0.0 |
| Literary artists |  | 1 | 33.3 | 2 | 66.7 |
| Visual artists |  | 0 | 0.0 | 8 | 100.0 |
| Total |  | 2 | 13.3 | 13 | 86.7 |
| Musicians | 1951–1970 | 3 | 20.0 | 12 | 80.0 |
| Dancers |  | 1 | 12.5 | 7 | 87.5 |
| Literary artists |  | 1 | 8.3 | 11 | 91.7 |
| Visual artists |  | 3 | 30.0 | 7 | 70.0 |
| Total |  | 8 | 17.8 | 37 | 82.2 |
| Musicians | 1971–1990 | 2 | 15.4 | 11 | 84.6 |
| Dancers |  | 7 | 30.4 | 16 | 69.6 |
| Literary artists |  | 4 | 28.6 | 10 | 71.4 |
| Visual artists |  | 3 | 23.1 | 10 | 76.9 |
| Total |  | 16 | 25.4 | 47 | 74.6 |
| Musicians | 1991–2010 | 0 | 0.0 | 0 | 0.0 |
| Dancers |  | 0 | 0.0 | 1 | 100.0 |

*Source:* Indykator 2013.

primarily comprised individuals born between 1950 and 1970, encompassing
musicians, literary artists and visual artists. Notably, this demographic was
predominantly composed of women rather than men, with no instances of
unemployment detected among dancers. It is pertinent to emphasize that,
following the stringent eligibility criteria for survey participation, these
individuals likely experienced involuntary unemployment, signifying their
willingness to engage in gainful employment at prevailing market rates but
encountered difficulties in securing job opportunities, or they were engaged
in work devoid of monetary compensation.

The frequency of the answers across the professional groups and
genders is presented in Table 3.5.

In the course of the focus group interviews and during the survey
conducted in the metropolitan area of Warsaw, of which results were
representative, it turned out that the monitoring and analysing of
individuals practising artistic professions is insufficient. What is more,
those individuals very often did not have any management competencies,
which confirms and emphasises the necessity for the creation of a
support system for artists and creators in Poland.

*Table 3.5* The status of the unemployed in the last five years. N = 127

| | | Yes Number of answers (N) | Percentage (%) | No Number of answers (N) | Percentage (%) |
|---|---|---|---|---|---|
| Musicians | Woman | 1 | 8.3 | 11 | 91.7 |
| Dancers | | 0 | 0.0 | 26 | 100.0 |
| Literary artists | | 4 | 23.5 | 13 | 76.5 |
| Visual artists | | 1 | 25.0 | 3 | 75.0 |
| Total | | 6 | 10.2 | 53 | 89.8 |
| Musicians | Man | 2 | 10.0 | 18 | 90.0 |
| Dancers | | 0 | 0.0 | 7 | 100.0 |
| Literary artists | | 2 | 15.4 | 11 | 84.6 |
| Visual artists | | 1 | 3.6 | 27 | 96.4 |
| Total | | 5 | 7.4 | 63 | 92.6 |

*Source:* Indykator 2013.

### 3.1.5 *Artists' employers – challenges and incentives associated with hiring artists*

As employees, artists are perceived as a very diverse group. This diversity is connected with the area of artistic activity and the type of work rather than the profile of the employer. The key criterion is related to the individual or collective (team-like) character of creative activity. Individuality and uniqueness, fundamental for actual creativity, are also vital. On the one hand, some groups are described by employers as 'ideal employees,' since they are ready to make sacrifices for the sake of an idea (FGI2.3), but on the other hand, employers indicate their demanding nature (FGI2.4).

Irrespective of the character of the work, the problem that was indicated is the clear insufficiency of remuneration received by artists and creators. While talking about actors, one of the interviewees noticed that often, out of respect for theatre and the belief that television is a worse medium, actors expect very high rates while working for television, since if they have taken on a kind of hack work and decided to work for money, then the money should be good (FGI2.3). In the case of the other professions, there is an option to earn extra money by teaching others or being active in another way.

The employers participating in the survey raised an important topic of the artist manager: on the one hand, there was a discussion about the competencies of artists, i.e. the question if and to what extent they should be their own managers, but on the other hand, there was the question of the potential position and role of managers. These questions include both personality traits and marketing or negotiation skills as well as skills for the fostering of relations with others. According to the interviewees, though, the most important is 'an idea of oneself,' a vision of developing one's career. As noticed by one of the interviewees:

> I have the impression that in Poland either there are not enough specialists in creating personal brands of specific people, the ones that are really valuable individuals, or during their education, artists do not learn how to create an image of themselves. Often they have no time for that, because they are busy, working only. But this is also a very important element in education, to let these artists know how they can sell themselves. (FGI2.4; translation ours)

However, it is also important that artists appreciate the work of a manager:

> I look after an artist … put lots of work into his personal brand. Also money. I sent him, for instance, to some festivals in Belgium. He goes to this festival in Belgium, plays there, it is fantastic … he achieves success … And during this festival in Belgium he starts to get in touch with others without the knowledge of his impresario. Those people call and say, "Well, listen … it's ok, but you know … he isn't reliable." … He thinks he will gain something from that … . He loses his credibility, as he can't retain these contacts, because he doesn't know how to do it and so on … He makes it once, earns some money and then he is back again to square one. (FGI2.4; translation ours)

Motivations for employing artists were related mainly to employment situations other than the 'typical' ones, i.e. in cultural institutions. Employing artists for one-off events or performances happens very rarely in the case of both individual artists and more complex forms, e.g. purchasing the rights for a performance or sponsoring a theatre spectacle, which seems to be a matter of custom or tradition:

> I mean … there isn't still this sort of … this kind of tradition and I think that those companies still haven't … they aren't still at the level to (But do you mean a financial level or rather … ?) No, it's not about the financial level, it's about the intellectual level. (FGI2.4; translation ours)

Employing artists involves their function as creative workers rather than image-related functions, which is especially true in the case of visual artists (FGI2.4, FGI2.2).

Artists, despite the initial opinion about them being ideal employees, are, at the same time, often difficult employees, which often results from the attitudes instilled during the education process or from promoting a belief in uniqueness:

> each violinist in the first year of primary school starts and believes that he or she will be a soloist. We do not have an education similar to the one they have elsewhere, I mean, they teach chamber musicians, orchestra musicians, and so on. Here, we educate only soloists. And then comes all of this frustration, which in the case of an orchestra results from the fact that ... (FGI2.4) that they are just the background, right? (FGI2.1). "Yes, I'm just part of the background and I was to ... I was educated to be a soloist." "I wanted to be a soloist." Many of them are simply frustrated people, because they can't believe ... (FGI2.4; translation ours)

The most important remark in connection with the artist's work refers to the incredible, according to the interviewee, level of preparation of musicians when performing other professions, especially professions that require concentration, discipline and a good memory. This is accompanied by the belief expressed by the artist that the attitudes and general competencies developed in the process of mastering the profession of a musician are a valuable resource for artists, allowing them to achieve success also in disciplines completely unrelated to music if only there is sufficient readiness to abandon music for another career (FGI2.4).

The Warsaw-Bydgoszcz survey helped to indicate problems and offered a preliminary view of the situation of artists in the labour market in Poland, which served as an impulse to further research, and in effect, to initiate works on introducing legal changes for the sake of artists in Poland. The conclusion from the research on the labour market of artists and creators in Poland (Ilczuk 2013) was as follows: 63% of the working artists participating in our survey assessed the state's support for artists as bad or very bad. Considering the other results obtained from the survey, it sounds like the so-called SOS signal sent by artists. The response to this signal should lead to the creation of such systematic solutions for the artists' labour market that will make its functioning efficient and artist-friendly.

## References

Begg, D., Fisher, S., & Dornbusch, R. (1993). Ekonomia, vol. 2. Państwowe Wydawnictwo Ekonomiczne, Warszawa.

Ilczuk, D. (2013). Rynek pracy artystów i twórców w Polsce. *Raport z badań.* Bydgoszcz–Warszawa: Ministerstwo Kultury i Dziedzictwa Narodowego.

Ilczuk D., Gruszka-Dobrzyńska E., Socha Z., Hazanowicz W. (2020), Policzone i policzeni! Artyści i artystki w Polsce, Wydawnictwo Uniwersytetu SWPS – Dom Wydawniczy Elipsa, Warszawa.

# 4 The professional situation of artists and creators

## Nationwide survey (2018)

### 4.1 Research method and sample

This survey, which was aimed at estimating the population size of artists, creators and performers in Poland in 2018, served as a basis for further research on systematic solutions which were recommended in 2013 and dedicated to this specific professional group. This research, although, was cross-sectional, carried out with the CAWI questionnaire, which is typical of quantitative research, and, as such, helped to glean knowledge about the situation of artists in the Polish market. The process of counting this group and the implications arising from their population size, which, as proven, is only seemingly large, are discussed in Chapter 6 of this monograph.

This 2018 survey was the second stage of the whole meta-survey, intended to obtain information about the situation and expectations of the research community and to offer more insights into the differences and similarities between particular industries and artistic and creative professions.

It should be emphasised that the survey confirmed that artists themselves support to a large extent the need for systematic solutions. Support for the introduction of a special legal solution that would be dedicated to professional groups of artists, creators and performers in Poland was expressed by 88% of the respondents. About 6% of the respondents were against the idea, and the same number did not know. The analysis of the answers reveals strong support for the suggested idea.

A great majority of the respondents, approximately 76%, stated that there is a need for creating collective rights that would be dedicated to artists; about 18% were of a neutral opinion about the idea and 8% did not agree with it.

Support for the introduction of a special social security contribution for artists, creators and performers in Poland was voiced by 87% of the respondents. The idea was rejected by 7%, while 6% had no opinion. Again, the results demonstrated strong support for the idea. Similarly,

DOI: 10.4324/9781003401032-5

the idea of regulating rates within and by the community in the labour market of artists, creators and performers was supported by 74% of the respondents. About 12% of the respondents were of a contrary opinion, whereas 14% did not hold any opinion. The analysis of the responses indicates strong support for the idea.

About 72% of the respondents were for the introduction of systematic mechanisms aimed at supporting artistic debuts; about 18% did not have a definite opinion and about 10% were against this solution. Support for the introduction of changes to the current system of access to artists' workshops or studios was voiced by approximately 55% of the respondents; 36% were of no opinion; and about 9% were against the idea (Ilczuk et al. 2020, p. 61).

The CAWI questionnaire was also aimed at verifying the adequacy of the catalogue of professions used in the survey. Since the research team did not have access to personal data from the databases analysed during the first stage of the research, which meant no possibility of random sampling (based on these databases) during the second stage, the team attempted to disseminate the information about the survey throughout the whole community of artists, creators and performers, i.e. in a group that is similar to the statistical population. The survey involved 5,019 individuals (which is the number of the completed questionnaires), including 2,643 men and 2,376 women, aged between 18 and 82, coming from 297 powiats, with a total number of 380 powiats in Poland.

The Computer-Assisted Web Interview is a technique for collecting data in market and opinion research, which involves filling in a questionnaire with the help of a computer. The questionnaire is made available on the Internet. It may be filled in by clicking on the link sent by researchers (in targeted recruitment projects) or by clicking on an advertisement banner that appears on Internet portals. The main advantage of using this technique is the time of receiving filled-in questionnaires, which are added to the database right after being completed. Accordingly, there is no time-consuming and costly process of coding questionnaires. In addition, the CAWI technique makes it possible to profile questions, i.e. to use filter questions as questions which open a wide set of more detailed issues.

It should be underscored that the questionnaire used in the research on estimating the population size of artists, creators and performers in Poland did not include questions about personal data, which would have allowed for an accurate identification of the respondents. However, according to relevant regulations of Polish law, a postal code, date of birth or the level of earnings were not considered personal data.

Using a CAWI-based research method guaranteed the anonymity of the survey. This was significant for several reasons. The professional group of artists, both men and women, is characterised by distrust.

The anonymity was provided and proven to create an atmosphere of safety and trust, which was catered for by the ambassadors of the survey uniquely: those were representatives of each artistic industry, the so-called research angels, including the writer Zygmunt Miłoszewski or the music manager Stanisław Trzciński.

What is more, the results of the questionnaires were aggregated based on the 'professions of artists, creators and performers.' The data received from the questionnaires were divided and classified into several independent sets and the research team did not analyse the content of each questionnaire. The analysis itself was conducted according to a set of specific questions, and if the respondent provided information about achievements, awards, etc, then the researcher did not know the responses to the other questions from the same questionnaire. What is more, the responses were covered by statistical confidentiality, and the data were not disclosed to any external parties, including the commissioner, at any stage of the research.

The questionnaire of the CAWI survey was divided into two parts. The first part included survey questions (dependent variables), while the second contained demographic data (independent variables).

## 4.2 Participants of the survey and their profile

The CAWI survey, which was carried out between 1 September and 10 November 2018, included 5,019[1] individuals representing all the indicated industries, i.e. film, literature, music, the visual arts, dance, theatre and folk art. Artists, creators and performers could choose one or more industries they represented in the questionnaire. That is why, 28% of the respondents indicated more than one industry, and the number of individuals representing each industry was greater than the total number of respondents. It follows, then, that there were two clearly separate categories of analysis included in the survey: the representatives of the industries and the respondents. The former included 6,848 individuals, and the latter 5,019.

What is important, the difference between the groups resulted from the multi-industry background of the respondents (e.g. a theatre and a film actor who also sings). In the case of analyses that required an individual approach to each respondent (e.g. earnings level, working time, etc.), the team decided to use the criterion of 'the main profession' to definitively classify an individual as a representative of a specific industry. Apart from this classification, which was created based on specially designed questions, there was also the procedure involving the industrial 'mapping' of specific professions.[2]

The number of respondents across the industries classified in terms of the main profession is demonstrated in Table 4.1.

*Table 4.1* Respondents and their industries according to their main profession in Poland in 2018

| Industry | N | % |
| --- | --- | --- |
| Visual arts | 1,327 | 26 |
| Music | 1,310 | 26 |
| Film | 832 | 17 |
| Literature | 754 | 15 |
| Theatre | 470 | 9 |
| Dance | 163 | 3 |
| Architecture | 86 | 2 |
| Interdisciplinary | 43 | 1 |
| Folk art | 34 | 1 |
| Total | 5,019 | 100 |

*Source:* own work.

In the survey sample, the industry of the visual arts had the greatest number of representatives (1,327 individuals); slightly fewer indicated music (1,310 individuals) and film (832 individuals). The industry of literature was represented by 754 individuals and theatre by 470 individuals. The industry of folk art and architecture was represented by the fewest individuals (34 and 86, respectively) (Ilczuk et al. 2020, pp. 34–35).

One of the first conclusions derived from the analysis of the responses was the fact that some artists, creators and performers worked in more than one industry. The phenomenon of interdisciplinarity or multi-professional index, which is discussed in more detail in Chapter 6.3, was true for more than a quarter of the survey sample (28%). Most frequently, the respondents would indicate only two industries (21%), though three industries were indicated by a statistically visible number (6%) (Table 4.2).

The fact that the respondents performed work in more than one industry allows us to look at the classification from a different angle.

*Table 4.2* The number of industries represented by the respondent in Poland in 2018

| Number of industries | N | % |
| --- | --- | --- |
| One industry | 3,443 | 72 |
| Two industries | 1,001 | 21 |
| Three industries | 267 | 6 |
| Four industries | 56 | 1 |
| Five and more industries | 9 | 0 |

*Source:* own work.

*Table 4.3* The number of individuals performing artistic, creative or performance work in a given industry understood as an area of activity in Poland in 2018

| Industry | N |
|---|---|
| Visual arts | 1,736 |
| Music | 1,529 |
| Film | 1,240 |
| Literature | 984 |
| Theatre | 867 |
| Dance | 264 |
| Folk art | 142 |
| Architecture | 86 |

*Source:* own work.

From this point of view, industries become 'areas of activity,' in which artists, creators and performers function. Table 4.3 presents the number of individuals who indicated a given industry as an area of their activity. While analysing the table, we should remember that the groups representing a particular number of representatives are not separate sets (Table 4.3).

The average age of the respondents taking part in the survey was 43: the number of the survey participants according to their age is illustrated in Table 4.4.

The largest segment of respondents fell within the age bracket of 30 to 39, constituting approximately 30% of the total respondents, equivalent to 1,462 individuals. The 40 to 49 age group was also notably represented, comprising roughly 22% of the respondents, amounting to 1,128 individuals. In contrast, the youngest and oldest segments were the least populous, with

*Table 4.4* Age ranges of the respondents in Poland in 2018

| Age range | N | % |
|---|---|---|
| Below 20 | 41 | 1 |
| 20–29 | 987 | 20 |
| 30–39 | 1,462 | 29 |
| 40–49 | 1,128 | 22 |
| 50–59 | 688 | 14 |
| 60–69 | 526 | 10 |
| 70–79 | 159 | 3 |
| Above 80 | 28 | 1 |
| Total | 5,019 | 100 |

*Source:* own work.

*Table 4.5* Average age of the respondents in Poland in 2018

| Industry | Women | Men | Total |
|----------|-------|-----|-------|
| Literature | 45 | 47 | 46 |
| Visual arts | 44 | 50 | 46 |
| Film | 43 | 47 | 45 |
| Folk art | 44 | 43 | 44 |
| Theatre | 41 | 42 | 41 |
| Architecture | 41 | 41 | 41 |
| Music | 37 | 39 | 39 |
| Dance | 34 | 34 | 34 |
| Total | 42 | 44 | 43 |

*Source:* own work.

less than 1% of respondents below the age of 20 (0.82%, or 41 individuals) and above the age of 80 (0.56%, or 28 individuals).

The average age of the survey participants across the professional groups was between 34 and 46 (of both women and men). As indicated in Table 4.5, on average, the oldest were the representatives of literature and the visual arts (46 years old in both cases), and the youngest, again on average, were the respondents in the industry of dance (34 years old). These results may be explained concerning the specifics of work performed in particular industries. Performing professions related to dance requires a better fitness level, which generally predisposes younger individuals to perform these jobs. Performing literary work or work related to the industry of the visual arts, on the other hand, certainly does not have to be associated with a young age.

The gender distribution was uneven, with a slight predominance of men. There were 267 more men than women participated in the study. There were 2,643 men and 2,376 women. Thus, men accounted for 53% of all the respondents, and women for 47% (a difference of 6% points). If we analyse the gender of the respondents across the industries, we can observe the largest disproportion (in terms of gender) in the industry of dance, with a predominance of women (192 women, as against 72 men). Men, on the other hand, significantly outnumber women in the sectors of film (482 women and 758 men) and music (533 women and 996 men) (Table 4.6).

The respondents came from the whole territory of Poland. There were representatives of all voivodeships and a great majority of Polish powiats (297 out of 380, which makes up 78%). Geographical data about the place of residence of the respondents indicated a correlation with the population size of particular administrative units in Poland.

Table 4.7 demonstrates the responses of the survey participants to the question, 'Who do you feel you are in terms of profession?' The respondents

*Table 4.6* Respondents across the industries according to their gender in
Poland in 2018

| Industry | Women | | Men | |
|---|---|---|---|---|
| | *N* | *%* | *N* | *%* |
| Dance | 123 | 75 | 40 | 25 |
| Interdisciplinary | 30 | 70 | 13 | 30 |
| Folk art | 22 | 65 | 12 | 35 |
| Literature | 451 | 60 | 303 | 40 |
| Visual arts | 742 | 56 | 585 | 44 |
| Architecture | 44 | 51 | 42 | 49 |
| Theatre | 231 | 49 | 239 | 51 |
| Film | 301 | 36 | 531 | 64 |
| Music | 432 | 33 | 878 | 67 |
| Total | 2,376 | 47 | 2,643 | 53 |

*Source:* own work.

could indicate several answers at once. The representatives of the dance
industry most frequently identified themselves as artists (83%), as was the
case with most of the representatives of music (78%), theatre (74%) and the
visual arts (68%), as well as a large group of the representatives of folk art
(64%). A great majority of the respondents of each industry identified
themselves as creators, i.e. 89% in literature, 88% in architecture, 82% in
film, 68% in the visual arts, 64% in folk art, 64% in theatre, 54% in dance
and 50% in music. The response 'performer' was indicated by a large group
of the representatives of music (62%), dance (50%), theatre (44%) and folk
art (43%).

The difference in terms of professional identity between the representatives of each industry should be highlighted. In dance and music,

*Table 4.7* Professional identity of the respondents in Poland in 2018

| Industry | Artist | Creator | Performer | None |
|---|---|---|---|---|
| Architecture | 0.35 | 0.88 | 0.19 | 0 |
| Film | 0.5 | 0.82 | 0.25 | 0.01 |
| Literature | 0.32 | 0.89 | 0.16 | 0.02 |
| Music | 0.78 | 0.5 | 0.62 | 0.02 |
| Visual arts | 0.68 | 0.68 | 0.2 | 0.01 |
| Dance | 0.83 | 0.54 | 0.5 | 0.03 |
| Theatre | 0.74 | 0.65 | 0.44 | 0.01 |
| Folk art | 0.64 | 0.68 | 0.43 | 0.02 |
| Total | 0.6 | 0.67 | 0.32 | 0.02 |

*Source:* own work.

there were mainly artists. In the visual arts, folk art and theatre, there were as many artists as creators, whereas in literature, film and architecture, there were mainly creators. Creators were most frequently indicated by musicians and dancers (see Table 4.7).

It should be noted that being a member of an organisation in the industry was not very popular among the survey sample. It was reported by less than 40% of the respondents. The largest percentage of membership in industry associations was among architects (over 80%), which is obviously related to the fact that the profession of an architect is a regulated profession, with chambers of architects granting the appropriate qualifications (Ilczuk et al. 2020, p. 40). A high percentage of membership was also observed among filmmakers (50%), followed by the representatives of the visual arts (43%) and literary artists (42%). The lowest percentage was observed among the representatives of the dance industry (18%) and folk artists (25%). Table 4.8 presents more detailed data.

In this context, age is a crucial independent variable. A cross-analysis of the responses and this variable indicates a specific tendency: the older the respondent was, the more likely he or she was to be a member of an organisation. This may be explained by reference to a model common to sports, where players ending their careers work in various organisations (the so-called sports activists) and focus on training younger generations and organising their training processes. Younger representatives of the community, on the other hand, do not have time to be engaged in the activities of industry organisations, since they are focused on performing their work; and if they want to achieve the best results possible, they have no time for other activities. Another hypothetical explanation of this situation is the lack of an interesting offer on the part of industry organisations aimed at younger generations of artists and creators.

It is also true that membership in industry associations is slightly more frequent in the case of men. It was indicated by 45% of men and 37% of women. It was similar in the case of the 'unionization' of the surveyed communities: 5% of men and 4% of women indicated they belonged to a union. However, at the same time, women indicated that they were more often involved in activities related to non-governmental organisations (see Table 4.9).

A great majority of the respondents representing specific industries had completed a higher arts education. However, owing to the specific character of the educational path, often different from the one observed in the case of the other professions, literary artists were an exception, since a great majority of them did not obtain arts education. A similar situation was observed among the representatives of folk art. Table 4.10 presents more detailed data.

*Table 4.8* Membership of the respondents in organisations in Poland in 2018

| Industry | Professional organisation of artists and creators | Other organisation of professionals | Association in the industry | Other non-governmental organisations (associations, foundations, etc.) | No membership in any organisations |
|---|---|---|---|---|---|
| Architecture | 0 | 0 | 0.83 | 0.07 | 0.16 |
| Film | 0.06 | 0.01 | 0.5 | 0.09 | 0.42 |
| Literature | 0.02 | 0.03 | 0.42 | 0.11 | 0.49 |
| Music | 0.07 | 0.03 | 0.36 | 0.1 | 0.51 |
| Visual arts | 0.01 | 0.01 | 0.43 | 0.13 | 0.49 |
| Dance | 0.03 | 0.02 | 0.18 | 0.2 | 0.63 |
| Theatre | 0.12 | 0.03 | 0.34 | 0.34 | 0.47 |
| Folk art | 0.01 | 0.02 | 0.25 | 0.27 | 0.53 |

*Source:* own work.

*Table 4.9* Gender of the respondents and their organisation membership in Poland in 2018

| Gender | Professional organisation of artists and creators | Other organisation of professionals | Industry association | Other non-governmental organisations (associations, foundations, etc.) | No membership in any organisations |
|---|---|---|---|---|---|
| Women | 0.04 | 0.02 | 0.37 | 0.11 | 0.52 |
| Men | 0.05 | 0.02 | 0.45 | 0.1 | 0.45 |

*Source:* own work.

*Table 4.10* Arts education of the respondents across the professions in Poland in 2018

| Industry | No (%) | Primary (%) | Secondary (%) | Higher (%) |
|---|---|---|---|---|
| Architecture | 32.2 | 5.3 | 21.2 | 41.3 |
| Theatre | 20.7 | 3.0 | 10.7 | 65.6 |
| Visual arts | 30.2 | 7.0 | 11.7 | 51.1 |
| Film | 71.7 | 1.7 | 3.6 | 23.0 |
| Music | 32.5 | 2.3 | 8.4 | 56.8 |
| Dance | 27.3 | 1.9 | 6.6 | 64.2 |
| Folk art | 47.2 | 4.2 | 14.1 | 34.5 |
| Literature | 19.8 | 2.3 | 1.2 | 76.7 |
| Total | 36.3 | 3.3 | 8.2 | 52.2 |

*Source:* own work.

Across all of the analysed industries, a greater majority of the respondents completed higher education (about 83% of the representatives of all of the industries, including 100% of the representatives of architecture, over 91% of the representatives of literature, over 87% of the representatives of theatre, over 85% of the representatives of the visual arts and over 82% of the representatives of film). Education at the secondary level was obtained by about 16% of the representatives of all of the industries together (including most of the representatives of folk art, i.e. about 33%, about 24% of the representatives of music and around 22% of dance). Education at the primary level was reported by the fewest number of the representatives of the industries (0.2% of the representatives) and so was education at the lower secondary level (0.4% of the representatives of all the industries). (Table 4.11)

*Table 4.11* General education of the respondents across the industries in Poland in 2018

| Industry | Primary | Lower secondary | Basic vocational | Secondary | Higher |
|---|---|---|---|---|---|
| Architecture | | | | | 1 |
| Literature | 0.002 | 0.003 | 0.001 | 0.079 | 0.915 |
| Theatre | | 0.005 | 0.007 | 0.115 | 0.873 |
| Visual arts | 0.003 | 0.002 | 0.005 | 0.138 | 0.852 |
| Film | 0.002 | 0.002 | 0.007 | 0.161 | 0.83 |
| Dance | | 0.008 | 0.011 | 0.224 | 0.758 |
| Music | 0.003 | 0.009 | 0.013 | 0.235 | 0.739 |
| Folk art | | | 0.021 | 0.331 | 0.648 |
| Total | 0.2% | 0.4% | 0.8% | 15.6% | 83.0% |

*Source:* own work.

Analysing the labour market of artists allows us to observe its many distinctive features. One of them is the level of education of its representatives, which is beyond average (Baumol, Throsby and Jeffri 2004). Research on the artists' labour market done around the world indicates that this professional group has education beyond the average level (Zawadzki 2016, pp. 124–125). As demonstrated by Rhys Davies and Robert Lindley (2003, p. 12), in the first decade of the 21st century in Great Britain, the number of artists with higher education alone was twice as high as the number of individuals with higher education in the general population. The same trend prevails in Poland, which is confirmed by the research carried out by Ilczuk and her team: in 2018, as many as 83% of individuals performing work in the arts had completed a higher education.

What is interesting is that higher arts education was obtained by slightly more than half of all the artists, creators and performers participating in the survey, i.e. 58%. Zawadzki (2016, p. 124; translation ours) writes that 'International research shows that despite the relatively low barriers to enter the artistic labour market in terms of formal qualifications, artists are a group of individuals with above-average education when compared to the total workforce.' This applies to, e.g. actors and directors. In the case of the latter, the level of education is one of the highest. Among theatre directors alone more than 83% of the respondents had a higher arts education, as made evident in the 2018 survey by Ilczuk and her team. Zawadzki notes, however, that those low market entry barriers are often related to formal qualifications, which does not translate into a low level of difficulties when an individual begins to work in the artistic profession.

The level of education among dancers is exceptionally high in the world. This was noted by Baumol, Throsby and Jeffri (2004) during their international research on the career transition of dancers. The collected data were very important for the dance industry, as they related mainly to the challenges of career transition. That was the first research of this kind; moreover, it was conducted in eleven different countries. The researchers pointed to the discrepancies between the expectations of young dancers entering the labour market and of those individuals who were coming to the end of their careers. It also turned out that actors and dancers are a group having education above average. The British survey conducted in 2005 by the Arts Council also proves that the number of individuals with higher education is higher among dancers than among all artists (Zawadzki 2016, p. 125).

As proven by the survey carried out by Ilczuk in 2018, Polish ballet dancers, who took part in the CAWI survey, in most of the cases had

*Table 4.12* Citizenship of the respondents in Poland in 2018

| Citizenship | N | % |
|---|---|---|
| Polish | 4,941 | 98.5 |
| Polish and other | 53 | 1.0 |
| other | 25 | 0.5 |

*Source:* own work.

general higher education (55%). However, this level is lower than the general level of the representatives of the dance industry, where as many as 76% had completed a higher education. Secondary education was obtained by 41% of individuals related to ballet and 4% most probably had not completed secondary school with a positive result on the final matura exam, which meant they had completed ballet school at the level of basic vocational education. Still, the survey indicates a positive trend: more than half of young individuals completing ballet schools success-fully pursue education at a higher level despite their professional workload (Table 4.12).

Almost the whole population of artists, creators and performers taking part in the survey had Polish citizenship (more than 98%). Among the 5,019 correctly completed questionnaires, 78 respondents indicated that they had 'Polish and other' citizenship or 'other' citizenship (around 1.5% of the survey sample). Table 4.13 presents the exact numbers of the respondents having citizenship other than Polish, or having Polish and other.

*Table 4.13* Other citizenships of the respondents in Poland in 2018.

| Citizenship | N |
|---|---|
| French | 10 |
| American | 9 |
| Canadian | 7 |
| German | 6 |
| Ukrainian | 5 |
| Belarusian, Dutch, Israeli, Russian, Swedish | 4 |
| British, Czech | 3 |
| Slovene, Italian | 2 |
| Croatian, Spanish, Lithuanian, Macedonian, Norwegian, Swiss, Silesian, Turkish, Venezuelan, Hungarian, both Italian and French | 1 |
| Total | 78 |

*Source:* own work.

### 4.3    Income, working time and the forms of employment

The question about monthly net income[3] in the last three years was answered by 4,770 individuals, which makes up 95% of the survey sample. The median monthly net earnings in this group amounted to PLN 2,500, approximately EUR 586.85.[4] It means that half of the artists, creators and performers taking part in the survey earned less than PLN 2,500 (EUR 586.85) net per month, which situates these professional groups close to the national average of the whole labour market.[5] The average monthly net earnings in the survey sample amounted to PLN 3,352, i.e. EUR 786.85. The most frequently declared income was PLN 3,000 net (509 individuals), followed by the amount of PLN 2,000, i.e. EUR 704.22 (446 individuals), PLN 2,500, i.e. EUR 586.85 (362 individuals) and PLN 4,000, i.e. EUR 938.97 (337 individuals). The difference between the median and the average (the average was higher by PLN 852, or EUR 200, than the median) shows that the respondents would frequently indicate earnings above the median value. In statistics, this phenomenon is called right-skewed asymmetry, and it tells us that the greater part of the population is below average. There were 651 individuals earning more than twice this amount (more than PLN 5,000 or EUR 1,173.71), which makes up 12.97% of all the respondents. There were 6.85% of affluent individuals[6] among the artists, creators and performers taking part in the survey (i.e. 344 individuals)[7] (Table 4.14) (Figure 4.1).

The analysis of earnings across the industries indicated a large degree of diversity. The industry which definitely stood out was film, where the median value of net earnings was PLN 4,000 or EUR 938.97 (the average amounting to PLN 5,132, or EUR 1,204.69). This was also the industry with almost half of the best-earning creators and performers taking part in the survey (315 individuals). The other end of the continuum was the dance industry and the visual arts (PLN 2,000, or EUR 586.85), as well as folk art, with a median value at the level of PLN 1,100, or EUR 258.21 net and a slightly higher average, which should be considered very low earnings. (Table 4.15)

Among the artists, creators and performers taking part in the survey, there was a significant variation in earnings across the genders. On average, women earned significantly less than men (by PLN 800, or EUR 187.79, net per month in the case of the median values and by PLN 1,150.18, or EUR 269.99, in the case of the average). Table 4.16 presents the gross earnings of women and men across the individual industries.

The top ten and the last ten professions in each industry were also indicated: in the first case, there was a clear predominance of professions from the film industry, whereas in the second case, one can note professions from the visual arts industry (Tables 4.17 and 4.18).

*Table 4.14* Median and average monthly earnings across the industries in Poland in 2018

| Industry | Net median | | Net average | | Gross median | | Gross average | |
|---|---|---|---|---|---|---|---|---|
| | PLN | EUR | PLN | EUR | PLN | EUR | PLN | EUR |
| Film | 4,000 | 938.97 | 5,132 | 1,204.69 | 4,396 | 1,031.92 | 5,593 | 1,312.91 |
| Architecture | 3,000 | 704.23 | 3,932 | 923.00 | 3,515 | 825.12 | 4,337 | 1,018.08 |
| Music | 2,800 | 657.28 | 3,294 | 773.24 | 3,141 | 737.32 | 3,759 | 882.39 |
| Literature | 2,500 | 586.85 | 3,235 | 759.39 | 3,141 | 737.32 | 3,637 | 853.76 |
| Theatre | 2,500 | 586.85 | 3,143 | 737.79 | 2,857 | 670.66 | 3,549 | 833.10 |
| Visual arts | 2,000 | 469.48 | 2,586 | 607.04 | 2,637 | 619.01 | 2,928 | 687.32 |
| Dance | 2,000 | 469.48 | 2,442 | 573.24 | 2,198 | 515.96 | 2,851 | 669.25 |
| Interdisciplinary | 1,700 | 399.06 | 2,354 | 552.58 | 1,851 | 434.51 | 2,756 | 646.95 |
| Folk art | 1,100 | 258.22 | 1,531 | 359.39 | 1,287 | 302.11 | 1,721 | 403.99 |
| Total | 2,500 | 586.85 | 3,353 | 787.09 | 3,000 | 704.23 | 3,742 | 878.40 |

*Source:* own work.

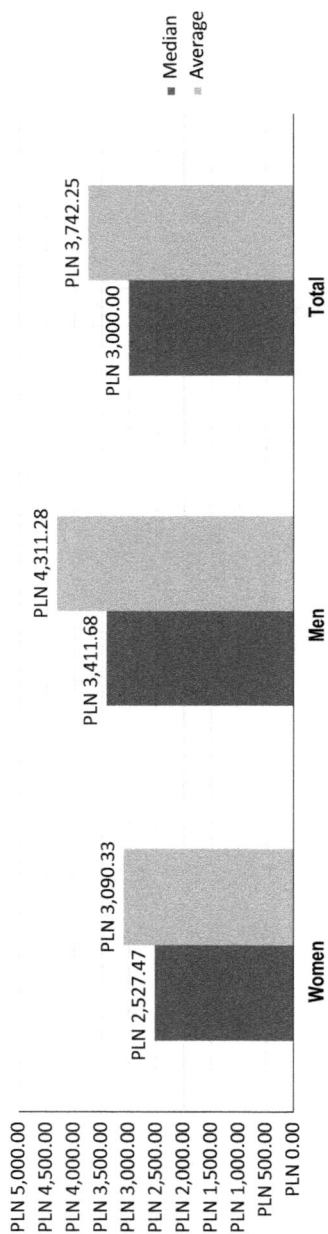

*Figure 4.1* Median and average values of gross monthly earnings of the respondents in Poland between 2016 and 2018.

*Source:* own work.

*Table 4.15* Net earnings across the industries and the gender of the respondents in Poland in 2018

| Industry | | Women | | Men | | Total | |
|---|---|---|---|---|---|---|---|
| | | *PLN* | *EURO* | *PLN* | *EURO* | *PLN* | *EURO* |
| Dance | Median | 2,000 | 469.48 | 2,150 | 504.69 | 2,000 | 469.48 |
| | Average | 2,502 | 587.32 | 2,232 | 523.94 | 2,442 | 573.24 |
| Theatre | Median | 2,500 | 586.85 | 3,000 | 704.23 | 2,500 | 586.85 |
| | Average | 2,863 | 672.07 | 3,417 | 802.11 | 3,143 | 737.79 |
| Music | Median | 2,500 | 586.85 | 3,000 | 704.23 | 2,800 | 657.28 |
| | Average | 2,591 | 608.22 | 3,643 | 855.16 | 3,294 | 773.24 |
| Literature | Median | 2,500 | 586.85 | 3,000 | 704.23 | 2,500 | 586.85 |
| | Average | 2,977 | 698.83 | 3,622 | 850.23 | 3,235 | 759.39 |
| Film | Median | 3,000 | 704.23 | 5,000 | 1,173.71 | 4,000 | 938.97 |
| | Average | 4,186 | 982.63 | 5,672 | 1,331.46 | 5,132 | 1,204.69 |
| Visual arts | Median | 1,880 | 441.31 | 2,500 | 586.85 | 2,000 | 469.48 |
| | Average | 2,146 | 503.76 | 3,142 | 737.56 | 2,586 | 607.04 |
| Folk art | Median | 800 | 187.79 | 1,500 | 352.11 | 1,100 | 258.22 |
| | Average | 1,212 | 284.51 | 2,082 | 488.73 | 1,531 | 359.39 |
| Architecture | Median | 2,800 | 657.28 | 3,600 | 845.07 | 3,000 | 704.23 |
| | Average | 3,729 | 875.35 | 4,168 | 978.40 | 3,932 | 923.00 |
| Total | Median | 2,200 | 516.43 | 3,000 | 704.23 | 2,500 | 586.85 |
| | Average | 2,748 | 645.07 | 3,900 | 915.49 | 3,352 | 786.85 |

*Source:* own work.

## 4.4 Social stratification – Gini index

In her book, which is based on the population size research of artists and creators, Ilczuk (2020) refers to the category of social stratification in terms of earnings, listed by Throsby (2010, p. 10). It was in 2020 that she wrote that the artists' labour market is an area 'where income is insecure and irregular, though it may reach a very high level' (Ilczuk et al. 2020, p. 11; translation ours).

An indicator informing about the stratification of earnings is the Gini coefficient, i.e. an index of social inequality. Its value ranges from 0 to 1, with 0 standing for full equality and 1 meaning the opposite: absolute inequality. In Poland in 2017, the index was 0.292. In 2021, it was 0.272. As argued by Ilczuk, the index calculated for the artistic community in Poland indicates a great stratification between individuals with the highest earnings and those with the lowest:

In the analysed industries of culture, the index was 0.44, which should be interpreted as indicative of greater inequalities within these industries than in Poland in general. Visible differences in terms of stratification of income across the specific industries were observed. It may be also stated

Table 4.16 Gross earnings across the industries and the gender of the respondents in Poland in 2018

| Industry | | Women | | Men | | Total | |
|---|---|---|---|---|---|---|---|
| | | PLN | EURO | PLN | EURO | PLN | EURO |
| Dance | Median | 2,000 | 469.48 | 2,747 | 644.84 | 2,198 | 515.96 |
| | Average | 2,378 | 558.22 | 3,449 | 809.62 | 2,851 | 669.25 |
| Theatre | Median | 2,747 | 644.84 | 3,297 | 773.94 | 2,857 | 670.66 |
| | Average | 3,276 | 769.01 | 3,960 | 929.58 | 3,549 | 833.10 |
| Music | Median | 2,830 | 664.32 | 3,297 | 773.94 | 3,141 | 737.32 |
| | Average | 3,025 | 710.09 | 4,124 | 968.08 | 3,759 | 882.39 |
| Literature | Median | 2,928 | 687.32 | 3,457 | 811.50 | 3,141 | 737.32 |
| | Average | 3,308 | 776.53 | 3,959 | 929.34 | 3,637 | 853.76 |
| Film | Median | 3,493 | 819.95 | 5,000 | 1,173.71 | 4,396 | 1,031.92 |
| | Average | 4,614 | 1,083.10 | 6,151 | 1,443.90 | 5,593 | 1,312.91 |
| Visual arts | Median | 2,618 | 614.55 | 2,685 | 630.28 | 2,637 | 619.01 |
| | Average | 3,018 | 708.45 | 2,620 | 615.02 | 2,928 | 687.32 |
| Folk art | Median | 800 | 187.79 | 1,648 | 386.85 | 1,287 | 302.11 |
| | Average | 1,351 | 317.14 | 2,361 | 554.23 | 1,721 | 403.99 |
| Architecture | Median | 3,000 | 704.23 | 4,127 | 968.78 | 3,515 | 825.12 |
| | Average | 3,986 | 935.68 | 4,744 | 1,113.62 | 4,337 | 1,018.08 |
| Interdisciplinary | Median | 1,072 | 251.64 | 4,948 | 1,161.50 | 1,851 | 434.51 |
| | Average | 1,848 | 433.80 | 4,782 | 1,122.54 | 2,756 | 646.95 |
| Total | Median | 2,527 | 593.19 | 3,412 | 800.94 | 3,000 | 704.23 |
| | Average | 3,090 | 725.35 | 4,331 | 1,016.67 | 3,742 | 878.40 |

Source: own work.

*Table 4.17* Net median earnings per month of selected professions: the top ten professions in Poland in 2018

| Profession | Median | Average |
|---|---|---|
| Colourist | PLN 8,000 (EUR 1,877.93) | PLN 9,961.54 (EUR 2,338.90) |
| Other film artists | PLN 5,000 (EUR 1,173.71) | PLN 5,252.17 (EUR 1,232.90) |
| Director of photography | PLN 5,000 (1,173.71 EUR) | PLN 5,998.48 (EUR 1,408.09) |
| Sound mixer | PLN 5,000 (1,173.71 EUR) | PLN 5,037.74 (EUR 1,182.57) |
| Film editor | PLN 5,000 (1,173.71 EUR) | PLN 6,060.20 (EUR 1,422.58) |
| Film set designer | PLN 4,750 (EUR 1,115.02) | PLN 8,041.67 (EUR 1,887.72) |
| Film scriptwriter | PLN 4,000 (EUR 938.97) | PLN 4,586.76 (EUR 1,076.70) |
| Scriptwriter | PLN 4,000 (EUR 938.97) | PLN 5,916.33 (EUR 1,388.81) |
| Sound director | PLN 4,000 (EUR 938.97) | PLN 4,680.00 (EUR 1,098.59) |
| Theatre stage designer | PLN 3,900 (EUR 915.49) | PLN 4,650.00 (EUR 1,091.55) |

*Source:* own work.

that this level of the index is typical of systems where there is a low degree of state interventionism in culture. (Ilczuk 2020, p. 51; translation ours)

In the case of the dance industry, the Gini coefficient was 0.370 in 2018 (Ilczuk et al. 2020, p. 51). This is one of the most equality-skewed values among the nine cultural industries included in the survey. In terms of equality, architecture has the best value (0.350), followed by dance and theatre immediately after. The worst result in terms of the equality of earnings was the one of folk art (which is also the smallest industry), where the coefficient was 0.565 in 2018, as well as the one of the interdisciplinary area and the visual arts (Table 4.19).

The regularity is associated with the period of work-related activity, observed in the age range between 30 and 60. According to the research findings, individuals belonging to this age cohort earn above average. There were also a number of cases of individuals with similar incomes outside this cohort. However, these were individuals of a senior age who were still active in the labour market. An analysis of the situation of individuals younger than the indicated cohort can help to indicate that, in general, the period of investing in an artistic career is long. Initially, there is a positive correlation between an increase in earnings and age, which disappears as the number of years of work-related activity increases.

When it comes to forms of employment, over half of all the respondents (in terms of the indicated professions) gained income from a contract for work, i.e. around 54% in terms of the represented professions (including almost 70% of the responses provided by theatre stage designers, jazz musicians, scriptwriters, directors of photography, make-up artists and burlesque artists; between 70% and 80% of the responses provided by

*Table 4.18* Net median earnings per month of selected professions: the last ten professions in Poland in 2018

| Profession | Median | Average |
|---|---|---|
| Sculptor | PLN 1,600 (EUR 375.59) | PLN 1,993.00 (EUR 467.84) |
| Contemporary dancer | PLN 1,500 (EUR 352.11) | PLN 1,411.04 (EUR 331.23) |
| Other musicians | PLN 1,500 (EUR 352.11) | PLN 1,787.60 (EUR 419.62) |
| Painter | PLN 1,500 (EUR 352.11) | PLN 1,942.40 (EUR 455.96) |
| Circus artist | PLN 1,500 (EUR 352.11) | PLN 1,830.00 (EUR 429.58) |
| Weaver | PLN 1,200 (EUR 281.69) | PLN 6,400.00 (EUR 1,502.36) |
| Church organist | PLN 1,200 (EUR 281.69) | PLN 2,108.33 (EUR 494.91) |
| Folk artist | PLN 1,100 (EUR 258.22) | PLN 1,531.00 (EUR 359.39) |
| Performance artists | PLN 950 (EUR 223.00) | PLN 1,633.23 (EUR 383.39) |
| Burlesque artist | PLN 600 (EUR 140.85) | PLN 820.00 (EUR 192.49) |

*Source:* own work.

theatre directors, playwrights, chamber musicians, audiovisual translators, film directors, film scriptwriters, film editors, film set designers, costume designers, animators, illustrators, colourists; and over 80% of the responses provided by literary translators, film actors and dubbing actors). Almost 11% of the representatives of particular professions reported that they had gained income under a contract for service and 14% based on self-employment. Almost 30% of the representatives of particular professions gained income without any contract (including 80% of the responses provided by interdisciplinary artists; between 50% and 60% of the responses provided by organists, poets, painters, performance artists, folk artists, burlesque artists and circus artists) (Table 4.20).

*Table 4.19* Gini coefficient calculated for gross earnings across the industries in Poland in 2018

| Industry | Gini coefficient for gross earnings |
|---|---|
| Architecture | 0.3501 |
| Interdisciplinary | 0.5056 |
| Dance | 0.3697 |
| Film | 0.4066 |
| Theatre | 0.3959 |
| Literature | 0.4118 |
| Music | 0.4265 |
| Folk art | 0.5646 |
| Visual arts | 0.4656 |
| Total | 0.4427 |

*Source:* own work.

*Table 4.20* Forms of employment of the respondents across selected professions in Poland in 2018

| Profession | Employment contract for a non-definite period of time | Employment contract for a definite period of time | Contract of service | Contract for work | Self-employment | No contract | other |
|---|---|---|---|---|---|---|---|
| Film actor | 0 | 0.03 | 0.08 | 0.8 | 0.11 | 0.05 | 0,02 |
| Theatre actor | 0.24 | 0.04 | 0.16 | 0.6 | 0.07 | 0.14 | 0.04 |
| Architect | 0.24 | 0.03 | 0.07 | 0.28 | 0.51 | 0.07 | 0.06 |
| Fine-arts photographer/ photographer | 0.07 | 0.02 | 0.12 | 0.45 | 0.21 | 0.38 | 0.08 |
| Painter | 0.06 | 0.02 | 0.06 | 0.31 | 0.09 | 0.56 | 0.11 |
| Choreographer | 0.05 | 0.04 | 0.15 | 0.64 | 0.14 | 0.21 | 0.08 |
| Composer/author of musical works | 0.04 | 0.01 | 0.09 | 0.47 | 0.1 | 0.44 | 0.11 |
| Orchestra musician | 0.45 | 0.14 | 0.12 | 0.48 | 0.04 | 0.09 | 0.04 |
| Director of photography | 0.04 | 0.01 | 0.05 | 0.69 | 0.27 | 0.12 | 0.02 |
| Poet | 0.03 | 0.01 | 0.05 | 0.36 | 0.05 | 0.58 | 0.08 |
| Theatre director | 0.03 | 0.04 | 0.1 | 0.71 | 0.11 | 0.15 | 0.04 |
| Ballet dancer | 0.38 | 0.16 | 0.16 | 0.36 | 0.04 | 0.16 | 0.07 |
| Literary translator | 0.03 | 0 | 0.07 | 0.83 | 0.11 | 0.07 | 0.05 |
| Folk artist | 0.02 | 0.01 | 0.16 | 0.29 | 0.15 | 0.6 | 0.04 |

*Source:* own work.[8]

*Table 4.21* How many hours per week do you work?

| Industry | Total Work | Creative Work |
|---|---|---|
| Literature | 46 | 24 |
| Folk art | 46 | 18 |
| Music | 45 | 22 |
| Film | 45 | 22 |
| Dance | 45 | 19 |
| Visual arts | 44 | 20 |
| Architecture | 44 | 17 |
| Theatre | 43 | 19 |
| Total | 45 | 21 |

*Source:* own work.

The average working time per week of the respondents amounted to approximately 45 hours a week, including about 21 hours devoted to artistic work. By comparing the total average working time per week across the industries, it was stated (Ilczuk et al. 2020) that it amounts to about 43 hours on average per week among the representatives of the theatre industry and around 46 hours on average per week in the case of literary and folk artists. Greater variability in terms of the industries was observed in the average working time devoted to creative work per week, ranging from around 17 hours on average per week in the group of architects to around 24 hours on average per week in the case of literary artists (Table 4.21).

When analysing the relations between arts education and earnings, one can observe some kind of regularity. Having an arts education at a higher level turned out to be correlated with higher earnings, with the median at the level of PLN 2,700 net per month. On the other hand, no art education or an art education at the primary level translated to a median value of PLN 2,500 net per month. In this context, arts education at the secondary level yielded the worst results, with an amount of PLN 2,400 net per month (see Table 4.22).

*Table 4.22* Art education of the respondents and net earnings per month in Poland in 2018

| Art education | Number of individuals | Median earnings |
|---|---|---|
| None | 1,825 | 2,500 |
| Primary | 164 | 2,500 |
| Secondary | 410 | 2,400 |
| Higher | 2,620 | 2,700 |
| Total | 5,019 | 2,500 |

*Source:* own work.

*Table 4.23* Gender of the respondents and working time in
Poland in 2018

| Gender | Total working time | Artistic working time |
|--------|--------------------|-----------------------|
| Women  | 42.90              | 20.57                 |
| Men    | 46.58              | 21.81                 |
| Total  | 44.83              | 21.22                 |

*Source:* own work.

It is no wonder that the best earnings were observed in those regions of the country that excel in terms of the economy. This referred mainly to the Mazowieckie and Wielkopolskie Voivodeships, where the earnings were the highest. The Małopolskie and Dolnośląskie Voivodeships followed. What was surprising was the low level observed in the Śląskie Voivodeship, which is one of the most heavily industrialised regions in the country.

The respondents indicated that they worked for about 45 hours per week, which means 5 hours more than the average working week in Poland, as stipulated in Article 129 of the Labour Code. However, they devoted only 47% of this time, i.e. 21 hours, to creative work. In the case of women, both results were lower, since they indicated 43 hours of work per week and 21 hours of creative work, whereas men indicated 47 hours in general and 22 hours of creative work (see Table 4.23). This discrepancy may be partially connected with the fact that, according to our research findings, men earned more than women.

## Notes

1 The number of complete and correctly filled-in questionnaires.
2 I.e. the procedure of classifying each profession to a specific industry, especially important in the case of multi-industry professions, such as e.g. stage designer, actor or director.
3 The research team decided to use net earnings, taking into account various forms of employment and at the same time the possibility of comparing the values; however, in the case of specific analyses, gross earnings were also presented (see Tables 4.14, 4.16, 4.19, 4.20 and 4.21). In order to arrive at gross values, the research team carried out a calculation procedure, taking into account the relevant form of employment indicated by the respondents. The differences between net and gross earnings, the so-called 'labour costs,' were calculated separately for each of the seven analysed forms of employment.
4 EUR 1 = PLN 4.26 according to the average exchange rate of the National Bank of Poland in 2018.
5 The median earnings in 2016 amounted to approximately PLN 2,512 net (around EUR 589.67; cf. A Biennial Report of Statistic Poland of 2017 on earnings in Poland).

6 According to a commonly accepted definition (used by e.g. KPMG or Deutsche Bank), these are individuals whose total income is above the second tax income threshold, i.e. PLN 85,528 (around EUR 20,077) in 2017.
7 Cf. gross average monthly earnings in Poland in October 2016 amounted to PLN 4,346.76 (around EUR 1,020.37; see *Struktura wynagrodzeń wg zawodów w październiku 2016 r.*).
8 The responses across the professions do not add up to 100%, since the question about the form of employment was multiple choice.

### References

Baumol, W. J., Jeffri, J., & Throsby, D. (2004). Making changes. Facilitating the transition of dancers to post-performance careers. Research Report, The aDvANCE Project, New York.

Cholewicka, E. (2023). Homo Saltatrix. Sytuacja kobiet na rynku pracy artystek i artystów baletu. Doctoral dissertation written under the supervision of Prof. Dorota Ilczuk and Dr. Sandra Frydrysiak at the Faculty of Humanities, SWPS University in Warsaw.

Davies, R., & Lindley, R. (2003). Artists in figures. *A statistical portrait of cultural occupations*. Warwick: University of Warwick.

Ilczuk D., Gruszka-Dobrzyńska E., Socha Z., & Hazanowicz W. (2020). Policzone i policzeni! Artyści i artystki w Polsce, Wydawnictwo Uniwersytetu SWPS – Dom Wydawniczy Elipsa. Warszawa.

Zawadzki, K. (2016). Praca i wynagrodzenie w gospodarce kreatywnej. Uwarunkowania-specyfika-ewolucja. Wydawnictwo Naukowe Uniwersytetu Mikołaja Kopernika.

# 5 Specific aspects of the labour market of artists and creators

## The example of performing arts

### 5.1 Gender dimension of the labour market of artists and creators in Poland

This chapter is devoted to the subject of women in the labour market of artists, exemplified and with special regard to the situation within the ballet and dance sector in Poland. This expertise was elaborated by Emilia Cholewicka for her unpublished doctoral dissertation defended in 2023 at SWPS University. She has been investigating Polish state ballet companies and the labour within this area.

Cholewicka argues after Throsby that talent is a category with no available tools of analysis, defying any empirical assessment. That was indicated by him in the list of specific features of the artists' labour market (Throsby 2001, pp. 110–112). However, as argued by Linda Nochlin, talent is culturally connected with the male-female dichotomy:

> the so-called woman question, far from being a minor, peripheral, and laughably provincial sub-issue grafted on to a serious, established discipline, can become a catalyst, an intellectual instrument, probing basic and "natural" assumptions, providing a paradigm for other kinds of internal questioning, and in turn providing links with paradigms established by radical approaches in other fields. (Nochlin 1971, p. 2)

Nochlin published a well-known essay under the title 'Why have there been no great women artists?' She addresses the problem of myths and, according to her, an incorrect attitude to the title question and an equally incorrect attempt made to answer it. She indicates that it is the discourse common to art history, feminist critique and academic debate that is responsible for the way female artists are depicted, i.e. as an exception against the background of male Artists having Talent and Genius. The research conducted by Ilczuk and her team has also demonstrated gender-based disproportions in artistic professions in the 21st century.

DOI: 10.4324/9781003401032-6

The Polish choreographer Teresa Kujawa had similar observations in the 1970s, stating that such an attitude towards female creators mythologizes the person of the female Artist as an individual with masculine features (Berski 1979). Such discourse fed into inequalities favouring male artists over female artists. It is 'the conditions generally productive of great art,' as argued by Nochlin (1971, p. 7), that impact the situation of female artists:

Behind the most sophisticated investigations of great artists – more specifically, the art-historical monograph, which accepts the notion of the great artist as primary, and the social and institutional structures within which he lived and worked as mere secondary "influences" or "background" – lurks the golden-nugget theory of genius and the free-enterprise conception of individual achievement. (Nochlin 1971, p. 9)

In 2013, the German painter Georg Baselitz, in an interview for the German magazine *Der Spiegel,* explained that there are only a few female painters because the market verifies their work. According to him, female painters paint worse pictures, losing the market battle against more talented male painters. His words, which presented an incorrect viewpoint (Gørrill 2020), only confirmed the theses formulated by Nochlin. However, if we assume that in the art world women and men are equal, then why are there still so few female artists? Nochlin provides the following answer:

The question tolls reproachfully in the background of most discussions of the so-called woman problem. But like so many other so-called questions involved in the feminist "controversy," it falsifies the nature of the issue at the same time that it insidiously supplies its own answer: "There have been no great women artists because women are incapable of greatness." (Nochlin 1971, p. 2)

Nochlin continues her argument, claiming that the use of the example of female artists who are a part of art history, followed by the attempt to prove that seemingly there is gender 'equality' has had, in fact, a negative effect. The reasons for the lack of female artists should be uncovered in a broader context beyond a feeling of satisfaction derived from the existence of excellent, yet still singular, examples of female artists, i.e. both historical figures and contemporary artists who often have had to abandon their femininity in favour of masculine qualities to adapt to the prevailing rules of the game in the patriarchal labour market.

Moreover, women face a great many obstacles in their professional development, including also the sphere of culture and the arts, which make the glass ceiling hanging over them even more unbreakable. Harmful cultural prejudices are one of the most solid elements of the joists that support this ceiling (Wilson 2014).

In the 1970s, Nochlin was making representation against such existing dependencies. The story of the world-famous choreographer Bronisława Niżyńska confirms Nochlin's insights and extrapolates them from the visual arts community to dance, as pointed out by Early:

> Crucially, she was a woman in a man's job—one of the very few women choreographers to have had the artistic and financial resources of a major ballet company at her disposal. Ninette de Valois is reported to have said that all choreographers are men 'except Nijinska, and she was a man really. (Early 1977, 17 in Burt 2007, pp. 91–92)

Though in terms of numbers, dance is denoted by a strong feminine presence in the area of creation, men tend to dominate in the sphere of i.e. choreography and management, including individuals leading dance troupes (especially in ballet) around the world. It is not only talent that stands behind the success of male choreographers and other creators (Nochlin 1971, 7–8).

The political, social and cultural situation, as well as financial resources or the infrastructure, all have had an influence on the success, or lack thereof, of female artists. This was observed in the 1990s by Christy Adiar when she analysed the situation in England. She points to the fact that the level of financing as well as its sources are the key factors influencing dancers, choreographers and dance companies, further adding that decreases in public spending on the arts may hinder artistic creativity. As a result, the kind of works that are created will remain 'safe,' i.e. in line with the policy and ideology of those in power, which will dole out depleted funds to favoured artists (Adair 1992, pp. 20–21).

The sense of feminist thought as well as the importance of women's work should be analysed also in the context of the commonly discussed problem of sustainable development, which up till 2015 was limited to environmental issues, with no consideration being given to gender equality or cultural values, which are becoming less and less distinctive in the context of globalisation. Linda Scott refers to a survey done by the consulting company Mckinsey, as well as reports by the WHO and the FAO, which indicate that women are currently responsible for producing around 40% of the world's GDP. Their share increased in 2015 to 37% and is still increasing. Soon, it will reach the level of equality, with women and men producing 50% of the GDP each (Scott 2021, pp. 55–56).

The survey done by Ilczuk and her team in 2018 included 5,019 individuals, i.e. 2,376 women and 2,643 men. The gender distribution was therefore close to equal, with a slight predominance of men (267). They accounted for 53% of all the respondents, and women for 47% (a difference of 6% points). In terms of numbers, women were the most numerous group in the following industries: dance (77% of women), folk art (63% of women) and the visual arts (59%). Music (35% of women) and film (39%) were the least feminised industries. In the case of architecture, the gender distribution leaned slightly towards women (51%), but it was still close to parity.

The survey by Ilczuk from 2018 proved that female artists are usually better educated: 90% of them had a higher general education and 58% had a higher arts education. Among male artists, the values were 77% and 47%, respectively (Ilczuk 2020, p. 44). At the same time, it is women who earn much less than men in artistic professions. On average, the difference amounts to PLN 800 net per month when we consider the median value and PLN 1,152 considering the average (Ilczuk 2020, p. 47). The subsequent section of the chapter discusses these differences in more detail.

It should be highlighted that the situation of female artists as well as of the relationships and differences between both genders is similar to the general trend observed in the labour market (Magda 2020), where gender is correlated with higher education: it is women who are better educated. The situation of women in the labour market in Poland is not favourable. The statistics have remained unchanged for years: the average professional activity of women in Poland is lower than in the European Union (63% as against 68%, respectively). Women pursuing professional careers are mainly women with higher education, aged 25–49, as shown by Iga Magda in the report about increasing the work-related activity of women in Poland (Magda 2020). Currently, almost 45% of working women have a higher education; by contrast, the largest group of working men are individuals with basic education (GUS 2018).

What should be also noted is the falling number of working women of the working age population between 2011 and 2017. The number fell by 79,000. At the same time, the number of working men rose by 90,000 (GUS 2018). The activity of the female part of society within the labour market depends mainly on their level of education, place of residence and their number of children (if any) and their age. According to the data from Statistics Poland, 16.5% of women work part-time because they are taking care of children. Increasing the professional activity of women is crucial for the functioning of the state simply because of the demographic challenges we are facing, and, indeed, the ineffective social security system. However, public policy does not support women, particularly mothers and women over 60.

The differences mentioned above are visible in an analysis of the education and gender of the respondents. In the case of higher education, the overall percentage of women with a higher education was 89.6, whereas in the case of men it was lower by over 12% points and reached the level of 77.03%. More men had a secondary education, i.e. 21.3% as compared to 9.3% of the female respondents (see Table 5.1).

*Table 5.1* General education of the respondents and their gender

| Gender | Primary | Lower secondary | Basic vocational | Secondary | Higher |
|---|---|---|---|---|---|
| Women | 0.002 | 0.004 | 0.006 | 0.093 | 0.896 |
| Men | 0.003 | 0.004 | 0.01 | 0.213 | 0.77 |

*Source:* own work.

*Table 5.2* Arts education of the respondents and their gender

| Gender | None | Primary | Secondary | Higher |
|---|---|---|---|---|
| Women | 0.307 | 0.027 | 0.088 | 0.578 |
| Men | 0.414 | 0.038 | 0.076 | 0.472 |

*Source:* own work.

In the case of arts education, there was a similar tendency. Again, the result was higher for women (69%) and lower by around 11% points in the case of men (58%). As for higher arts education, the results were 58% and 47%, respectively (Table 5.2).

Considering the working week across all of the analysed artistic industries, women worked a total of 43 hours (including 21 hours of creative work). The result was lower than that for men, who on average worked for 47 hours (including 22 hours of creative work; Ilczuk 2020, p. 56). The results confirm the general tendency among the working population: women work less than men, usually because of culture-dependent roles of taking care of children and household duties (Magda 2020; Scott 2020).

### 5.1.1 Gender gaps

A gender gap is an effect of a number of processes, stereotypes and mental burdens that systematically lower the chances of girls and women, at different stages of their lives, to develop their talents and innate abilities. (Szwiec and Zawora 2020, p. 4; translation ours)

#### 5.1.1.1 Gender pay gap

The gender pay gap is a measure indicating the discrepancies across remuneration between men and women who work. If there is a particularly large gender pay gap among employees, it may mean that there are a number of issues that need to be examined and individual calculations can help to understand them. The gender pay gap is different from equal pay. Equal pay is a statutory requirement for employers, according to which it is illegal to pay men and women differently if they perform the same work, similar work or work of equal value (Global Gender Gap Report 2022). In addition, the unadjusted and the adjusted pay gaps are two different measures. The unadjusted pay gap is the average gender pay gap. In Poland in 2019, it was 8.5%, according to Eurostat calculations. It means that Poland ranks relatively high in the gender equality classification. After its adjustment, i.e. taking into account the percentage difference between women and men working in the same position, the gender pay gap was as much as 17% in 2019. According to the reports prepared by Statistics Poland, the level of the adjusted gender pay gap has not changed much for years: it has rather fluctuated, ranging from 17% to 19.9% (Magda 2020).

The gender pay gap is influenced by a great many factors. Firstly, it is related to the context of motherhood and its consequences i.e. stereo-types and the still prevailing patriarchal culture, which forces women into specific roles related to unpaid care work. In addition, women more often work part-time and decide to take longer leave, which is related to raising children. What is more, as Magda (2020) indicates, women are less likely to occupy highly paid positions, and so feminised industries are usually industries with lower average earnings (see also Noble 1992). The private sector is characterised by a greater gender pay gap when compared to the public sector. Moreover, the higher the position is, the greater the gender pay gap becomes. The gender disproportion is visible also in the level of old-age pension benefits, of which the amount is directly related to the overall period of performing work: over 15% of old-age pensioners are at risk of poverty in Poland, with women receiving on average old-age pensions benefits lower by 18.7% when compared to men.

The gender pay gap in the cultural and creative sectors is strictly connected with the low number of women holding higher positions. Apart from that, the artistic work of women seems to be less appreciated and has a lower value in the market when compared to that of men. This means that, in addition to the pay gap, women also receive lower remuneration and less recognition for their work. These factors, as well as the fact that women are subject to gender stereotypes and are less likely to experience vertical career growth, make access to the full artistic labour market more limited for women in the cultural and creative sectors. This is a point made by the authors of the report *Gender Gaps in the Cultural and Creative Sectors* (2022, p. 103). Examining the industries as a whole, we can see that the largest pay gaps to the detriment of women occur in the fields of the visual arts (39%) and film (26%). The smallest disproportions in the remuneration of women and men are found among individuals connected with theatre (7%) and dance (15%). It should be noted that there is no industry in which the average earnings of women would be higher than those of men.

In 2018, the highest pay gap occurred in the professions of curator, illustrator, interior designer, colourist, academic teacher in the field of the arts and theatre pedagogue. Professions in which women earn more than men, and the ones where women were not the only respondents, include weaver, film set designer, scriptwriter, film producer and stage designer.

The most equal professions in terms of the gender pay gap are theatre actor, creative producer, ceramic artist (with men receiving higher earnings), choir singer, designer and deejay (with women receiving higher earnings). The difference in earnings in favour of men did not exceed PLN 200 in the case of the following professions: choir singer, designer in the field of industrial design and deejay. The difference in earnings in favour of women also did not exceed PLN 200.

### 5.1.1.2 *Access to the market*

Taking care of others is another factor influencing the access of female artists to the market. As indicated in the report *Gender Gaps in the Cultural and Creative Sectors* (2022, p. 30), professions in the cultural and creative sectors are based on freelance projects, which require flexibility and availability from employees. Such work also means an increased lack of stability and a sense of insecurity, which adversely relates to women bringing up children, looking after senior family members, and managing households.

The report mentioned above shows that when a woman employed in the creative sector gives birth to a child, she may find it very difficult to re-enter the labour market; and if she succeeds in doing so, she is likely to have a lower position than before giving birth (*Gender Gaps in the Cultural and Creative Sectors* 2022, p. 31). According to the authors of the report, this problem is a particular challenge in the architecture sector, with such a great level of competition that a few-month break from work negatively affects the position of individuals, mainly women, who decide to leave the sector temporarily. What is more, in all the sectors, it is assumed that women will work less, be less focused, less flexible and less dedicated when they start having children. This was particularly evident in both the music and visual arts sectors (*Gender Gaps in the Cultural and Creative Sectors* 2022, p. 31). Similarly, in dance and ballet, there is a high degree of competition, especially in the case of women. In addition, the hourly system of work in a ballet company makes it impossible to take care of children at the earliest stages of their lives, while pregnancy, due to the specifics of work as a ballet dancer, which is described in the subsequent sections, automatically excludes women from the possibility of performing work that could pose a threat to the health of the developing child. There is also no possibility of part-time work: being part of the company means being ready to take on any role and play any part.

Moreover, women surrounded by men in managerial positions experience a phenomenon referred to as 'the glass ceiling' (Williams 1992; Adams and Funk 2012; Powell and Butterfield 2015) and are unable to break through to reach the highest positions in cultural and art institutions. This is related to stereotypes regarding the division of roles between the genders that still prevail.

### 5.1.1.3   Managerial level

All the cultural and creative industries are characterised by a lower number of women than men in the area of management. Across different sectors and their sub-sectors, the situation is somewhat different, for example, in the field of museology and cultural heritage, as well as cultural education, women are quite well represented. According to the own research (Cholewicka 2021), as well as the report mentioned in the previous sections (*Gender Gaps in the Cultural and Creative Sectors* 2022, p. 27), in ballet, there are significantly fewer women responsible for decision-making than men, whereas in contemporary dance the converse obtains, with female choreographers and female directors of contemporary dance companies being in the majority.

Nevertheless, managerial and creative positions in the field of all the creative sectors and cultural industries are dominated by men. Again, to a large extent, this is the result of culturally conditioned, 'normalised' and harmful stereotypes and the division of professional and social roles.

### 5.1.1.4   Stigmatising stereotypes

As made evident by the authors of the report *Gender Gaps in the Cultural and Creative Sectors* (2022, pp. 25–27), there are many reasons that in a stigmatising way influence the position of women in the field of culture and the arts as well as in the creative industries. They may be observed across all the cultural and creative sectors (CCS). A common trend is for men to more often hold more prestigious, decision-making and creative positions. They are more frequently the heads of prestigious cultural institutions that have commercial significance (even in the sectors where the absolute numbers of women are greater than those of men, such as dance and ballet).

It should be noted that the work of women is usually less valued and appreciated, compared to the work of men in the entire cultural and creative industries, which again results from cultural conditions and traditional mores.

## 5.2 Polish theatre artists during the COVID-19 pandemic

In the second half of 2020, the team of CBnGK at the SWPS University led by Professor Dorota Ilczuk, following the commission of the Zbigniew Raszewski Theatre Institute, carried out a survey about the situation of theatre artists during the COVID-19 pandemic (Ilczuk in cooperation with Karpińska, Cholewicka, Gruszka-Dobrzyńska, Piwowar, Socha, 2020). The primary objective was to investigate the socio-economic and professional circumstances during the economic lockdown. To obtain a comprehensive overview of the entire community, the research team opted for quantitative research using the CAWI method with a representative sample. It was determined that a representative sample should consist of 357 individuals, with a margin of error of 5%. Ultimately, 749 responses were collected. Nevertheless, only 541 questionnaires underwent analysis, specifically, those completed by individuals who indicated that between 2016 and 2019, at least half of their income had been derived from work within the theatre sector. The survey encompassed participants from 38 theatre-related professions, and these were further categorized into nine primary groups, including theatre actors, puppeteers, musical theatre actors, playwrights, stage designers, dance theatre dancers, ballet dancers, and other theatre artists, such as sound directors and makeup artists, for example.

### 5.2.1 *Professional situation of theatre artists during the pandemic: a quantitative survey*

The survey clearly showed the deteriorating situation of artists in the pandemic. In the case of all theatre artists, an income decrease of 54% was reported, from PLN 5,863.58, or approximately EUR 1,320.63, before the pandemic to PLN 2,687.36 (EUR 605.26) during the pandemic. Musical theatre actors suffered most from the pandemic, losing 77% of their income (from an average of PLN 6,836.61, or EUR 1,539.78, before the pandemic to PLN 1,553.73, or about EUR 349.94, during it), followed by directors with a loss of 64% and playwrights, whose earnings decreased by 61%. The situation of the other professional groups was far from optimistic. The smallest decrease in earnings was reported by ballet dancers; however, it still reached as much as 21%. The situation of artists turns out to be even more worrying when we realise that the average monthly salary in the business enterprise sector in Poland, without the payment of profit-based bonuses, in October 2020 amounted to PLN 5,456.24, i.e. EUR 1,228.88, according to the announcement of the Statistics Poland of November 19, 2020. None of the professional groups, apart from playwrights, reached such a level of earnings during the pandemic (Table 5.3).

So what did the artists participating in the survey do during this time to make ends meet? About 32% of the individuals said that they were supported by their relatives; slightly fewer (31%) indicated that they had

*Table 5.3* Average gross earnings per month before and during the pandemic
across the professions (N = 541)

| Profession | Average earnings before the pandemic | | Average earnings during the pandemic | | Decrease (%) |
|---|---|---|---|---|---|
| | PLN | EUR | PLN | EUR | |
| Musical theatre actors | 6,836.61 | 1,539.78 | 1,553.73 | 349.94 | −77% |
| Directors | 6,542.86 | 1,473.62 | 2,367.29 | 533.17 | −64% |
| Playwrights | 15,218.75 | 3,427.65 | 5,992.18 | 1,349.59 | −61% |
| Stage designers | 6,916.67 | 1,557.81 | 3,056.25 | 688.34 | −56% |
| Other theatre artists | 6,300.3 | 1,418.99 | 2,841.53 | 639.98 | −55% |
| Dramatic theatre actors | 5,169.21 | 1,164.24 | 2,684.35 | 604.58 | −48% |
| Puppeteers | 4,381.82 | 986.90 | 2,654.11 | 597.77 | −39% |
| Dance theatre dancers | 3,055.56 | 688.19 | 2,127.01 | 479.06 | −30% |
| Ballet dancers | 4,198.21 | 945.54 | 3,323.13 | 748.45 | −21% |
| **Total** | **5,863.58** | **1,320.63** | **2,687.36** | **605.26** | **-54%** |

*Source:* own work.

savings allowing them to survive for a maximum of three months; only 23%
of the respondents had savings allowing them to remain without work for a
longer period. As many as 30% of the respondents said they had no savings
at all. 41% of the respondents had loans, including 29% having a mortgage
on a house or flat and 12% having received a consumer loan. About 2% of
the respondents had another job and 1% decided to make a career transition
(Figure 5.1).

The decrease in earnings during the pandemic was also reflected in the
decreasing number of contracts. The researchers asked the respondents to
indicate the type of theatre they worked for and the type of contract they
had before and during the pandemic. The analysis did not lead to a precise
determination of the specific reasons for the loss of contracts. However, it
can be assumed that the pandemic was one of the reasons, if not the main
one. Moreover, the value of those contracts remains unknown. The data in
Figure 5.2 show the dynamics of employment in the labour market of
theatre artists at the time.

The greatest decrease in the number of contracts was observed in the
case of artists working for independent companies (46%), private theatre
companies (45%) and theatre companies run by non-governmental organisations (41%). A relatively low decrease (20%) was experienced by artists
working in private theatres, which, often thanks to subsidies, could offer full-
time employment contracts. Most frequently, it was contracts of service (56%)
and contracts for work (39%) that were terminated, since these are civil law
contracts that do not guarantee stable employment (Figure 5.3).

Due to the difficult economic situation of artists, various types of
support were introduced. The generally available 'anti-crisis shield' offered,

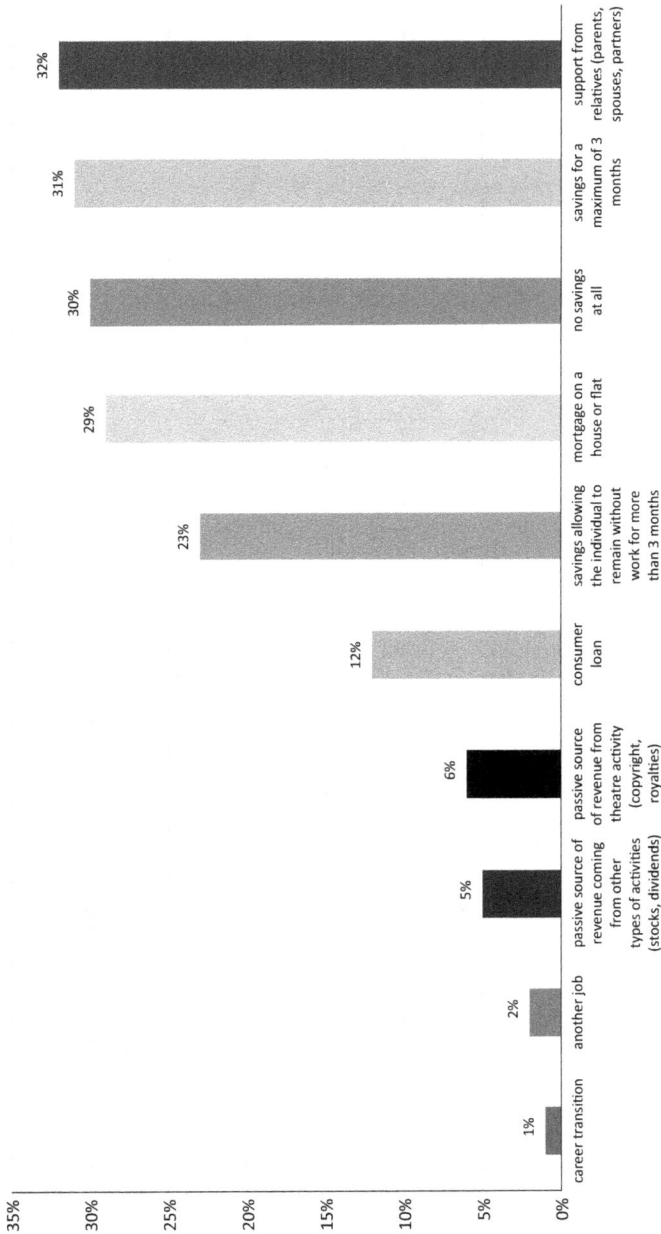

*Figure 5.1* Financial situation of theatre artists (N = 542, multiple choice).

*Source:* own work.

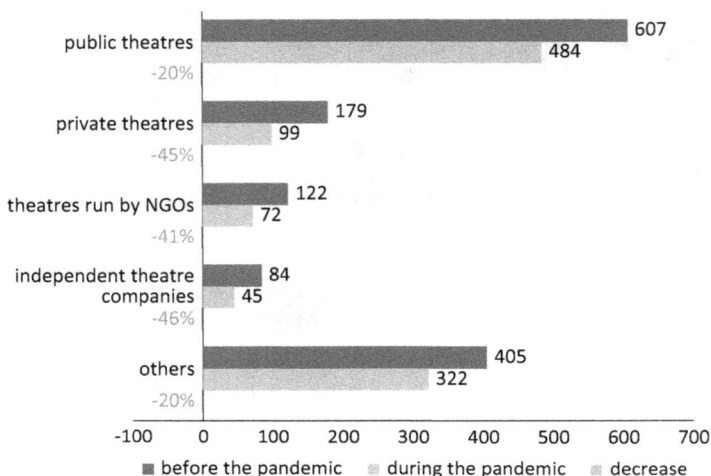

*Figure 5.2* Decrease in the number of contracts between March and October 2020 across various types of theatres (N = 541).

*Source:* own work.

for example, idle time benefits (three months of financial support for self-employed individuals and those working under contracts for work or contracts of service in the amount of 80% of the minimum wage) or loans for small and microenterprises. Support for artists was coordinated by the Ministry of Culture and National Heritage through various types of programmes. Unions and associations were involved in the support as well. More than half of the respondents (56%) decided to use various types of support, including mainly the financial one. It was most often used by musical theatre actors (80%), which is not surprising, considering that this group reported the highest decreases in remuneration. Ballet dancers (26%) used support least often. The most frequently used source of support was the Ministry of Culture and National Heritage, with 38% of the respondents taking advantage of its programmes. About 33% of the respondents used the anti-crisis shield. About 11% admitted that they received help from the artistic community and 10% from artistic unions and associations. Among the most frequently mentioned difficulties in applying for support, the respondents indicated a lack of adequate information (48%) and administrative difficulties (42%) (Figure 5.4).

Most theatre artists declared that they used online forms of artistic work during the pandemic. An affirmative answer was given by 74% of the respondents. All playwrights, 94% of puppeteers and 89% of theatre

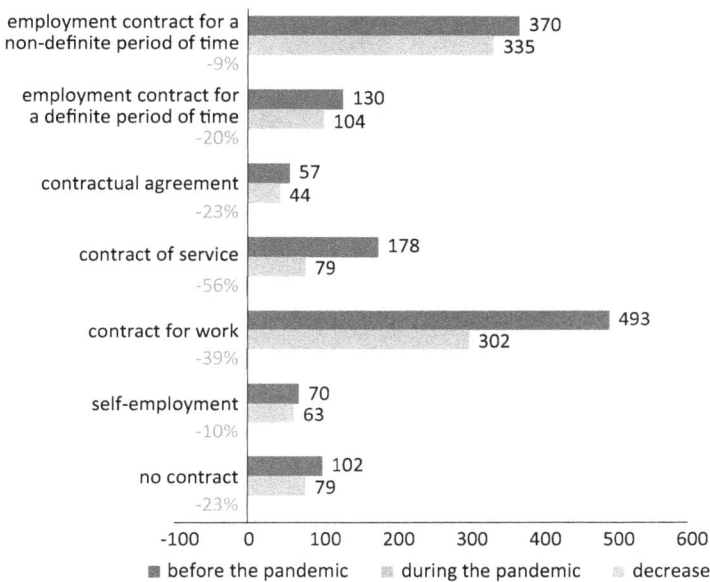

*Figure 5.3* Decrease in the number of contracts between March and October 2020
(N = 541).

*Source:* own work.

directors managed to work on online projects. This type of work proved
to be the most challenging for theatre stage designers: only 50% of the
respondents from this professional group managed to be engaged in such
an undertaking. The reasons for not performing work online included
the lack of possibilities to work in this way, lack of digital competencies,
lack of appropriate equipment, concern about the quality of artistic
activities, and the inability to build contact with the spectator. The
respondents also pointed out that their work was not suitable for
transference to the virtual sphere (Figure 5.5).

### 5.2.2  *Theatre artists and their professional situation during the pandemic*

The research team has wrapped up the statistical depiction of the artists'
circumstances by examining the responses to the optional open-ended
question. Despite its non-mandatory nature, 415 individuals voluntarily
provided their insights. These insights encompassed various aspects,
such as the challenges associated with online work, the pressure to halt

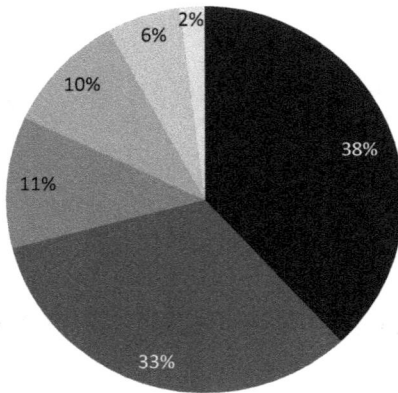

- ■ support of the ministry, e.g. the "Online Culture" programme
- ■ generally accessible support from the state (within the anti-crisis shield, e.g. idle time benefits, loans for small and microenterprises)
- ■ self-help (support from artistic communities)
- ■ support from artistic organisations and associations (including unions)
- ■ support from local authorities
- ■ support from private companies

*Figure 5.4* Sources of support used between March and October 2020 (N = 303).
*Source:* own work.

artistic pursuits, the struggle to maintain a standard of living and fulfil artistic requirements, assorted shortcomings like instability and the need for skill acquisition and education, contemplation of employment methods and the drawbacks of freelance work, and lastly, alterations in life goals and the need to embark on a career change.

- *My performances are being cancelled all the time. I was supposed to take part in several new productions that have been cancelled.*[1]
- *I haven't realised the planned performances and I haven't played in any performances for 5 months.*
- *I've missed about 100 performances.*
- *I'm wondering how I can make a career transition. I keep wondering whether the theatre as we know it will exist. Will it survive? Is this a matter of a year? 6 months? I'm currently at home, I have come out of isolation, I was supposed to play a crazy number this month: 7 performances. I won't play even one.*

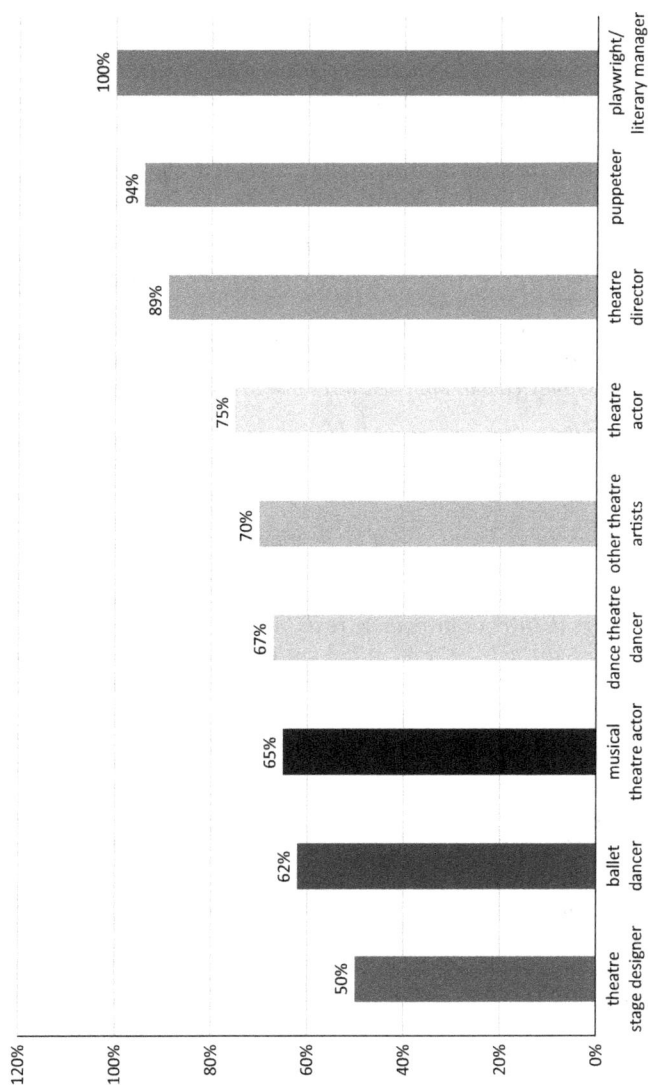

*Figure 5.5* Did you use any forms of online artistic work during the pandemic? (N=541, only affirmative answers).

*Source:* own work.

One of the commonly used words was '**lack**' (appearing twenty times), used in the context of the lack of: *prospects (creative, developmental, life), the possibility of moving ahead with plans, stability, premieres/ performances, and financial resources.*

- *The lack of systematic work and systematic performances in the profession of a dancer is problematic. It's hard to stay in shape, even working alone.*
- *Lack of prospects.*
- *Lack of performances = no spectators, no sharing of art, no creating emotions, no going on stage, no presenting Art!!!! No dance or movement classes!!!*

In numerous cases, the participants simply conveyed feelings of discouragement, despair, and various related challenges.

- *The pandemic has exposed the fragility of the entire system. Currently, I'm trying to direct my actions and professional plans towards survival. Nothing will ever be the same.*
- *The pandemic has prevented me from finding additional work in other theatres. Currently, the directors of other theatres cannot talk to new actors, because they cannot plan new hires due to the pandemic situation.*

*Yet, a portion of the respondents regarded the pandemic's circumstances as a transient challenge, something to be endured by engaging in alternative areas of endeavour or as a chance to explore fresh avenues for creative expression.*

- *As long as a premiere looms, I will be fighting.*
- *I still want to believe that everything will be normal again.*
- *Basically, I don't change my plans, apart from translating fewer artistic texts in favour of purely entertaining texts.*
- *It hasn't changed radically, I'm still doing what I was doing, but I'm trying to secure something for the future, guaranteeing myself the continuity of projects to a greater extent than before. Before the pandemic, it was easier to get into spontaneous projects.*

The survey served as a valuable tool in assessing the extent to which the professional and living conditions of theatre artists had been weakened by the COVID-19 pandemic. It emphasized the importance of collecting data on this professional group when planning new solutions, aligning with the hypothesis that there had been an insufficient level of monitoring of the artists' labour market in Poland. The impact of the pandemic was significant across all the professional categories included in the survey, as evidenced by income reductions of up to 77% compared to pre-pandemic levels. This was an alarming situation, especially when considered against the generally precarious financial state of the survey respondents. In this context, a critical concern revolved around the duration of the COVID-19 pandemic and how many more lockdowns and restrictions on cultural institutions would continue to affect this sector. Naturally, no one could have foreseen these developments, as the future always remains uncertain. Nevertheless, the survey underscored the importance of establishing stable regulations for the future operation of theatres. Such regulations, as indicated by the survey, form the only viable foundation for devising an appropriate strategy and implementing it at the individual theatre level. The focus should be on creating transparent conditions that enable theatres to function effectively (Ilczuk et al. 2021).

One of the attempts made to support theatres in this situation was the Culture Support Fund created by the Minister of Culture and National Heritage in 2020. The programme, which could draw on PLN 400 million (EUR 90.08 million) and was addressed to institutions, NGOs and enterprises operating in the fields of music, theatre and dance, was intended to mitigate the crisis in the creative economy sectors, which again corresponds to one of the theses presented in the Introduction, i.e. the one about the positive impact of the economic steering of the supply side of the artists' labour market. Unfortunately, the programme met with a substantial lack of positive reaction from the public and many negative comments. The most frequent accusations included the improper allocation of funds and biased decision-making in terms of the support it offered. This situation has exposed the lack of understanding and public support for individuals working in the cultural and creative sectors, not only artists and creators, but also specialists and technicians cooperating with them.

## Note

1 All of the responses to the open-ended question presented in the section were originally provided in Polish in Ilczuk, Karpińska and Socha (2021).

## References

Adair, C. (1992). *Women and dance: Sylphs and sirens*. Bloomsbury Publishing.

Adams, R. B., & Funk, P. (2012). Beyond the glass ceiling: Does gender matter?. *Management Science, 58*(2), 219–235.

Berski, J. (1979). *Rozmowa z Teresą Kujawą*. Miesięcznik Literacki.

Burt, R. (2007). *The male dancer: Bodies, spectacle, sexualities*. Routledge.

Cholewicka, E. (2021). Women to the placards! The socio-economic situation of female choreographers in the male world of ballet art. *Annales Universitatis Paedagogicae Cracoviensis| Studia de Cultura, 13*(2), 72–89.

Cholewicka, E. (2023) Homo Saltatrix. Sytuacja kobiet na rynku pracy artystek i artystów baletu. Doctoral dissertation written under the supervision of Prof. Dorota Ilczuk and Dr. Sandra Frydrysiak at the Faculty of Humanities, SWPS University in Warsaw.

Early, T. (1977). 'What Balletmakers was', *New Dance*, 2 (spring): 16–17.

Global Gender Gap Report (2022). World Economic Forum. [online] https://www.weforum.org/reports/global-gender-gap-report-2022/ [access: 19.04.2023].

Gørrill, H. (2020). Women Can't Paint: Gender, the Glass Ceiling and Values in Contemporary Art. Bloomsbury Publishing USA.

GUS (2018). Kobiety i mężczyźni na rynku pracy. [online] https://stat.gov.pl/obszary-tematyczne/rynek-pracy/opracowania/kobiety-i-mezczyzni-na-rynku-pracy-2018,1,7.html [dostęp 29.04.2019].

Ilczuk, D. in cooperation with Karpińska, A., Cholewicka, E., Gruszka-Dobrzyńska, E., Piwowar, K., & Socha Z. (2020). Artyści i Artystki Teatru w czasach COVID-19, Instytut Teatralny im. Z. Raszewskiego, Warszawa.

Ilczuk D., Gruszka-Dobrzyńska E., Socha Z., & Hazanowicz W. (2020). Policzone i policzeni! Artyści i artystki w Polsce, Wydawnictwo Uniwersytetu SWPS – Dom Wydawniczy Elipsa. Warszawa.

Ilczuk, D., Karpińska, A., & Socha, Z. (2021). Siła rażenia pandemii. Artyści i artystki teatru w świetle wyników badań ilościowych. [in] Teatr w pandemii, red. Kalinowska, K. Kułakowska, K. Instytut Teatralny im. Z. Raszewskiego, Warszawa.

Magda, I. (2020). Jak zwiększyć aktywność zawodową kobiet w Polsce. IBS Policy Paper, 1, 2020.

Nochlin, L. (1971). Why have there been no great women artists? UPenn Library [online] https://www.writing.upenn.edu/library/Nochlin-Linda_Why-Have-There-Been-No-Great-Women-Artists.pdf [access: 19.04.2023].

Nochlin, L. (2018). *Women, art, and power and other essays*. Routledge.

Powell, G. N., & Butterfield, D. A. (2015). The glass ceiling: What have we learned 20 years on?. *Journal of Organizational Effectiveness: People and Performance*.

Presley Noble, B. (1992). At work; and now the sticky floor. The New York Times. Retrieved from: http://www.nytimes.com/1992/11/22/business/at-work-and-now-the-sticky-floor.html.

Publications Office of the European Union (2022). Gender gaps in the cultural and creative sectors. In Publications Office of the European Union. LU: Publications Office of the European Union. Retrieved from https://op.europa.eu/en/publication-detail/-/publication/92d621d1-bb99-11ec-b6f4-01aa75ed71a1

Scott, L. (2020). *The Double X Economy: The Epic Potential of Empowering Women| A GUARDIAN SCIENCE BOOK OF THE YEAR*. Faber & Faber.

Szwiec, A., & Zawora, M. (2020). Gender Gapo po polsku. Raport z badania. Stowarzyszenia Women in Technology Poland. Kraków. [online] 11.2020: https://uploads-ssl.webflow.com/63b83afa6df4ef75243a1782/6404f43ae2cfd95812fb5e3c_Gender_gap_po_polsku.pdf [dostęp]: 29.04.2023.

Throsby, D. (2010). Ekonomia i kultura, tłum. O. Siara, Narodowe Centrum Kultury, Warszawa.

Throsby, D. (2001). *Economics and culture*. Cambridge University Press.

Vecco, M., Vroonhof, P., Clarke, M., van der Graaf, A., de Haan, A., Komorowski M., Asardag, D., & Milosavljević, M. (2019). [online] Gender gaps in the cultural and creative sectors, European expert network on culture and audiovisual (EENCA): https://eenca.com/eenca/assets/File/EENCA%20publications/Final%20Report%20-%20Gender%20in%20CCS%20EAC%20with%20Additional%20sections%20AV%20and%20Radio.pdf] [access 28.08.2022].

Williams, C. L. (1992). The glass escalator: Hidden advantages for men in the 'female' professions. *Social Problems, 39*(3).

Wilson, E. (2014). Diversity, culture and the glass ceiling. *Journal of Cultural Diversity, 21*(3), 83.

# 6 Estimating the number of working artists in Poland[1]

## 6.1 Research method and process

In 2020, a book entitled 'Policzone, policzeni. Artyści i artystki w Polsce' by D. Ilczuk, E. Gruszka-Dobrzyńska, Z. Socha and W. Hazanowicz was published. The book includes the results of a 2018 study dedicated to the process aimed at changing the legislation on artists in Poland (Ilczuk et al. 2020). It turned out that to introduce changes, it was necessary to estimate the number of individuals who would enjoy new rights. Without this knowledge, it was impossible to adequately estimate the financial dimension of the planned regulations. Although it seems a trivial matter, for many years, all efforts made by the artistic community to introduce rights dedicated to artists ended up being abandoned at the very initial stage, precisely because of the lack of data on the number of individuals professionally performing artistic and creative work. Ilczuk says:

> There was a popular belief that the size of the community is impossible to be determined, because it is mainly made up of freelancers, rather than full-time employees; the following phrase was often repeated, "Artists … who knows how many there are; and, generally, it is impossible to count them." In addition, the artistic community is diverse, and each profession, as we illustrated in the previous chapter, has specific characteristics. (Ilczuk and others 2020, cover page)

The CBnGK research centre at the SWPS University led by Ilczuk, having been commissioned by the Fryderyk Chopin Institute, made recourse to its own resources and research experience and decided to carry out research into the population size of artists in Poland as part of the study of which the results are presented in the previous chapter in the context of the professional situation of artists and creators. This research project was exploratory to a large extent and had not been conducted in such a scope in any scientific or statistical centres before; in fact, it was the first study of this type carried out in modern Poland. Even more so

DOI: 10.4324/9781003401032-7

after several years of analysing the issues of the artists' labour market, we can see how this situation clearly shows serious deficiencies in the monitoring procedure of the artists' labour market, which is again in line with our hypothesis.

In the second half of 2018, a series of studies were conducted to estimate the population size of artists, creators and performers across professional groups connected with the following industries: the visual arts, music, theatre, dance, film, literature and folk art. What is more, the research was aimed at stimulating the activity of the artistic community in the context of introducing systematic solutions for supporting artists and collecting detailed data which would allow for a systematic analysis of the survey population. The aims were achieved. The population of working artists, creators and performers was estimated at the level of 59,970 individuals (Ilczuk et al. 2020). The cover of the above-mentioned book reads:

It is not a large professional group. In the colloquial perception, artists seem to be more numerous, and the authors know what this is due to. This is influenced by the phenomenon of multiprofessionalism common in this group, a factor of 2.5 meaning that the group is estimated to be about 2.5 times larger. Isn't that interesting? (...) We present the first large-scale study of the size of the professionally active artistic community in post-war Poland. This pioneering research endeavour, not previously undertaken to such an extent in any science or statistics, was combined with a simultaneous recognition of the professional situation and opinions of this social group. (...) We approached this responsible task with great anxiety. In our wildest dreams, however, we could not have imagined that our survey would receive an overwhelmingly positive response from artists. More than 5,000 responses speak for themselves.

The survey included 600 entities, such as government agencies, public cultural institutions, associations of creators, trade unions of professionals, collective management organisations, independent non-governmental organisations, business entities and informal groups, all of which provided access to their databases and sent the questionnaire to their members (Ilczuk et al. 2020).

The object of research was the population size of individuals performing work that is commonly considered artistic or creative. The key to identifying them was their practised professions. Analysis of the secondary research data on the population size of artists was complemented by data harmonisation, i.e. making the data taken from different databases as comparable as possible and avoiding the risk of counting one individual multiple times. Work in the industries included in the survey was connected with multi-profession work, i.e. combining the artistic profession with a non-artistic one or practising several artistic professions. Because of that, the research process was complemented with a questionnaire survey. It helped to identify the scale of multi-professional work in the community, which is discussed in the final section of the chapter, and to recognise the professional situation of artists and their expectations concerning the support system. Thus, two simultaneous stages of the research were combined: the analysis of the secondary research data and a questionnaire survey, of which the results are discussed in more detail in the previous chapter of the book.

The initial assumption was that the research would include individuals who earn a living by performing creative or artistic work, and for whom this type of activity constitutes a very high portion of their household budget. More precisely, it meant applying the criterion defined for a professional artist, i.e. at least 50% of the overall income comes from artistic work (Throsby 2001; Ilczuk et al. 2013). Due to the specific character of their work, in the case of literary artists the criterion was 30%. However, in the course of the research, this criterion proved to be too exclusive. It was verified negatively after the opinions of organisations operating in the industries and the respondents had been taken into account. The population size research included all individuals reported by organisations operating in the industries as well as individuals self-reporting their professional activity as artistic, creative or performance-based.

The research method was a modified version of the original procedure of estimating the population size, which was verified positively in the research project of the Polish Music Council in 2016. The method was founded on several research assumptions connected with decision-making in the context of:

- operational definitions
- the category of professions (adding the smallest units, i.e. professions)
- sources of information in the process of creating databases
- the integration of various databases (a critical approach to sources based on their comparison).

The research process consisted of two main stages, i.e. estimating the population size and complementary research, demonstrated in Figure 6.1.

The first stage of the research included three types of work (meaning three subsequent research steps). During this stage, the rule of using at least two sources was followed. It meant that the population size of each profession was estimated based on at least two independent sources. The sources included databases of central institutions of the state and statistical offices (e.g. the Ministry of Family, Labour and Social Policy, Ministry of Finance, Statistics Poland, institutes of the Ministry of Culture and

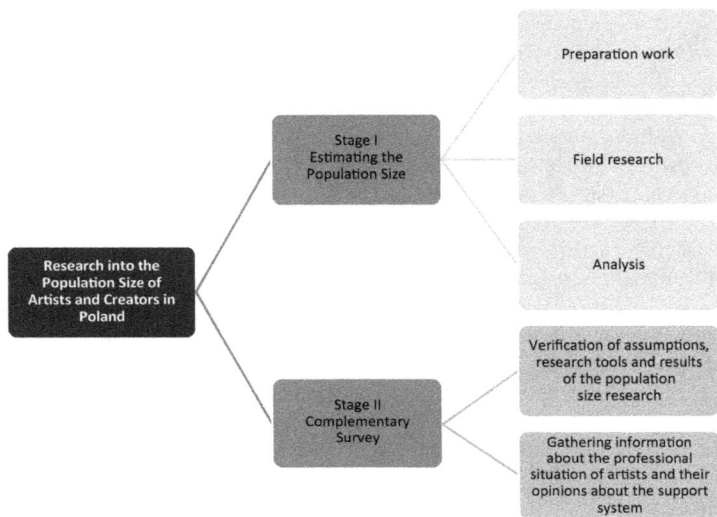

*Figure 6.1* The research process.
*Source:* own work.

National Heritage), data kept by artistic organisations (data on membership and community coverage from professional associations and unions) as well as data directly referring to the labour market (e.g. data on royalties obtained from collective management organisations, data from the National Library of Poland). Whenever possible, the fourth source, based on Internet data parsing, was also used. Thus, new databases were created, having been obtained from the existing Internet resources. In addition, in the industries that are more dispersed and less institutionalised (literature and the visual arts), manual counting of working artists was used (e.g. by aggregating data from the archives of art galleries in Poland about the seasons between 2016 and 2018) (Table 6.1).

The data from the first type of sources were obtained by sending official letters with a request for access to data about the number of individuals practising specific professions according to the Classification of Occupations and Specializations of the Ministry of Family, Labour and Social Policy. The data from the second type of sources, on the other hand, were obtained by the researchers, who had established direct contact with particular organisations. The data were obtained by telephone or email. Numerous in-depth conversations with representatives

Table 6.1 Sources of data on the industries/fields of the cultural sectors

| Industry | Data from central state institutions | Data from professional organisations and associations | Data from the labour market |
|---|---|---|---|
| **Film** | GUS, MF, MPiPS, PISF | SFP, PSM, PSC | talent and acting agencies, ZPAV, ZAPA |
| **Literature** | GUS, MF | UL, SPP, STL, ZLP | BN |
| **Music** | GUS, MF, MRPiPS, IMiT, IT | STOMUR, STL, SAWP, SPAM | ZAiKS, STOART |
| **Visual arts** | GUS, MF, MRPiPS, CEA | ZPAP | case study of the number of works of art exhibited in art galleries |
| **Dance** | GUS, MF, MPiPS, IT, IMiT | ZASP, PFT, PZTan, ZZAB | not applicable |
| **Theatre** | GUS, MF, MRPiPS, IT | ZASP, ZZAP | ZASP, talent and acting agencies |
| **Folk art** | GUS | STLu | not applicable |

*Source:* own work based on Ilczuk et al. 2020.[2]

of a great many organisations were an indispensable element of this research stage. In addition to collecting numerical data, those conversations facilitated the distribution of the questionnaire survey in the communities included in the research.

The third type of sources used to estimate the population size of artistic communities included mainly data taken directly from collective management organisations that deal with copyright and have information about the number of individuals who collect royalties. In cases where no information of this type was available, data about living book authors from the greatest collection in Poland (i.e. the one kept by the National Library) were used. There was also a separate study into the number of artists whose works had been exhibited in art galleries.

Analysing the process of estimation outlined in the book *Policzone, policzeni ...* (Ilczuk et al. 2020) we see that the first problem encountered by the research team run by Ilczuk was how to divide the community into industries. Initially, those were supposed to have been independent industries, i.e. the visual arts, literature, music, film, theatre, dance and folk art. In the course of the research, it turned out, however, that when we look at particular professions, the industries actually overlap, as is the case with a scriptwriter who can simultaneously work in the field of literature, film and theatre.

It was also one of the reasons why the artistic community seems so numerous. In the course of the research, it also became apparent that multi-professional work, or multi-professionalism, is a common phenomenon. It means that one individual becomes a representative of several groups and several different industries. Each artist, creator or performer practises 2.5 professions on average, which creates a misleading picture of the community.

To illustrate how the estimation process was made less ambiguous, let us consider the profession of a theatre actor. In the case of this profession, the estimation of the population size was done by Ilczuk (Ilczuk at al. 2020) in the following way:

- the estimated size based on the data obtained from community organisations: 8,000 individuals
- the estimated size based on the data from the Theatre Institute (the average number of members of acting companies multiplied by the number of companies, including private theatres): 8,800 individuals
- the estimated size based on data from Statistics Poland (the number of full-time jobs divided by the percentage of full-time employment in the profession): 7,350 individuals
- the reciprocal of the multi-professional index for the profession: 1.73
- the final estimated size: 4,250 individuals.

## 6.2  Research results

According to the research method, the results concerning the size of the population of artists, creators and performers obtained during the first stage of the research were verified with the help of the results of the complementary research (stage II), carried out simultaneously. That is why in the estimations presented below, the data is presented according to both the initial plan of dividing the artistic community into industries and professions and our own slightly modified approach to the question, which resulted from our experience of working with the community for months (including the questionnaire survey and consultations).

Based on the analysis of the secondary databases and numerous calculations done by the research team, it managed to obtain the first results about the estimated size of the population of artists and creators in Poland. Considering the initial definition and the professions included in the catalogue of creative and artistic professions, the number of artists, creators and performers in Poland was estimated to be 44,070 individuals, including 18,750 musicians, 10,330 visual artists, 5,525 theatre artists, 3,080 creators working in the film industry, 2,360 literary artists and authors, 2,250 dancers, 1,475 folk artists and 300 creators working interdisciplinarily.

In the course of the simultaneously conducted research during the first and second stage, the research team received many comments concerning the questionnaire, the range of industries and the professions included in the research. The catalogue of professions was an open set, which means it was open to be discussed and modified. As a result, the research team received many requests to include other professions in the catalogue. In the subsequent paragraphs, we present some of the recurrent requests concerning professions that may be easily classified and accurately described. Individuals representing professions that defy any classification were included in a separate category of 'other' professions, including professions of artists, creators and performers.

In the visual arts, the following professions were indicated as the ones that should be added to the catalogue: architect, ceramic artist, visual artist, illustrator, curator, graphic designer and comic illustrator. In the case of literature, the following were suggested: lyricist, journalist, opinion journalist, editor and reporter. In film, the following specialisations were suggested: animator, production manager and creative producer. The theatre-related communities suggested including the profession of a circus artist, literary manager and theatre producer. Representatives of the music industry suggested that the profession of an instrumental teacher and music producer be added. It was also suggested that the list of dance-related professions be updated with a burlesque artist. Folk art communities called for a different professional dimension of the industry, which, however, requires an in-depth separate discussion. Moreover, it was suggested that multi-industry or interdisciplinary professions be added, as their main feature encompasses at least two professions fully or in parts, a good example being a performance artist.

Analysing the outcomes of the research done in 2018, a significant procedure has been noticed. A majority of the suggested professions in the list have been added to the catalogue. The record was updated with the following professions:

• the visual arts: architect, ceramic artist, visual artist, illustrator, curator, graphic designer and comic illustrator
• literature: lyricist
• film: animator (animated films), colourist
• theatre: circus artist
• music: accompanist/tutor, music producer
• dance: burlesque artist
• interdisciplinary: performance artist (shifting the profession from the industry of the visual arts to the interdisciplinary sector).

Having considered other individual requests, the research team decided not to include professions related to arts and crafts,[3] which are not a part of folk art; however, at the same time, the contribution representatives of these professions have made to the development of artistic and creative communities was appreciated. The decision was driven by the fact that the field of arts and crafts falls within legal solutions which allow its representatives to avail of favourable treatment.[4]

An important area of activity of artists, creators and performers is their educational work. This conclusion was proven in the 2013 survey and confirmed in the 2018 survey of the population size, discussed here. Education is a frequent area of employment and one of the most obvious career paths for many artists, creators and performers. However, it was not included in the research catalogue in 2018. The reason for this was the practical impossibility of clearly separating the creative part from the area of formal and informal arts education, which is the basis of the research. At the same time, individuals performing artistic activities along with educational activities were included in relevant professions.

Table 5.3 presents detailed size estimations across the industries after the process of introducing the modifications presented above. According to the division, the size of the community was estimated to be **59,970 individuals**. The population was predominantly represented by music, with 19,100 individuals, and the visual arts, with an estimated number of 12,005 individuals. The least common industry, on the other hand, was folk art, which was estimated to have a population of 1,475 individuals practising professions belonging to this industry.

What is more, there is a special case of one of the industries not being included in the initial classification, i.e. architecture, that should be highlighted. It is worth noting that the community expressed a strong identity with the visual arts, and a greater majority of its representatives defined their work as creative. At the same time, the community is characterised by a different educational path and a strongly regulated labour market.[5] The fact that architects belong to the cultural sector was made absolutely clear by the Minister of Culture and National Heritage, who established The National Institute of Architecture and Urban Planning.[6] Considering the potential influence of this fact on the analysis and evaluation of the visual arts as a whole (with architects making up over 50% of the group population), the research team decided to treat architecture in further argumentation as the eighth industry (Table 6.2).

According to the findings, the cultural industries do not include individual communities, but rather they overlap to some extent, creating in this way a community that is both diversified and partially unified. A great majority of the industries have common elements with several other industries. Figure 6.2 gives a simplified overview of this fact.

The absolute numbers provided in the table refer to the category of the 'main profession' and cannot be treated as the overall numbers of individuals practising a specific profession. When considering the total population size in each profession, one has to remember about the multi-professionalism within artistic communities, mentioned on many occasions in this book and fully described below (Table 6.3).

*Table 6.2* Final population size estimates across the industries (with the new professions added to list of professions) in Poland in 2018

| Industry | Estimated size |
| --- | --- |
| Music | 19,100 |
| Architecture | 12,500 |
| Visual arts | 12,005 |
| Theatre | 5,750 |
| Film | 3,580 |
| Literature | 2,830 |
| Dance | 2,380 |
| Folk art | 1,475 |
| Interdisciplinary | 350 |
| Total | 59,970 |

*Source:* own work.

## Initial Division of Industries

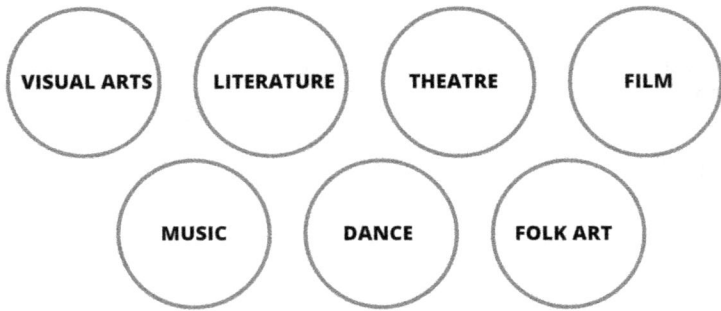

## Industries in Reality

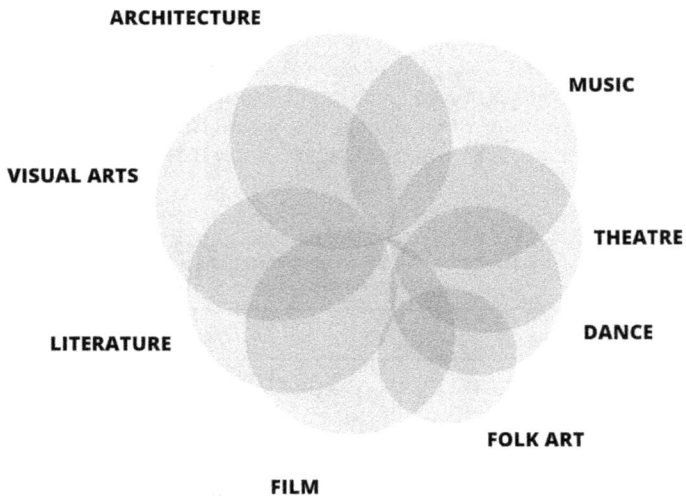

*Figure 6.2* Industries included in the research and their mutual overlap in Poland in 2018.

*Source:* own work based on Ilczuk et al. 2020.

*Table 6.3* Absolute population sizes across the professions in Poland in 2018

| Profession | Industry | Estimated size |
| --- | --- | --- |
| Accompanist/tutor* | music | 50 |
| Animator (animated film)* | film | 200 |
| Architect* | architecture | 12,5 |
| Architectural conservator | visual arts | 50 |
| Arranger (music) | music | 50 |
| Art conservator | visual arts | 100 |
| Audiovisual translator | literature | 150 |
| Ballet dancer | dance | 430 |
| Ballroom dancer***** | dance | 0 |
| Burlesque artist* | dance | 30 |
| Ceramic artist* | visual arts | 100 |
| Chamber musician | music | 1,2 |
| Chamber singer | music | 100 |
| Choir singer | music | 1,75 |
| Choreographer | dance | 200 |
| Church organist | music | 500 |
| Circus artist* | theatre / visual arts | 150 |
| Classical soloist | music | 300 |
| Colourist* | film | 100 |
| Comic illustrator* | visual arts | 200 |
| Commercial dancer | dance | 1,1 |
| Composer/author of musical texts | music | 1,2 |
| Computer game designer | visual arts | 150 |
| Computer graphic artist | visual arts | 3,6 |
| Conductor/band leader | music | 130 |
| Contemporary dancer | dance | 300 |
| Costume designer | film | 100 |
| Curator* | visual arts | 100 |
| Dance theatre dancer | dance/theatre | 200 |
| Deejay | music | 2,03 |
| Designer / industrial design | visual arts | 1 |
| Director of photography | film | 400 |
| Dubbing actor | film | 50 |
| Film actor | film | 980 |
| Film director | film | 750 |
| film editor | film | 500 |
| Film set designer*** | film / visual arts | 100 |
| Fine-arts photographer/photographer | visual arts | 1,05 |
| Folk /traditional musician | music/folk art | 250 |
| Folk artist | folk art | 1,35 |
| Folk dancer | dance | 120 |
| Graphic artist | visual arts | 400 |
| Graphic designer* | visual arts | 100 |
| Illustrator | visual arts | 400 |
| Illustrator* | visual arts | 300 |
| Interdisciplinary artists | interdisciplinary | 50 |
| Interior designer | visual arts | 1,5 |

*(Continued)*

*Table 6.3* (Continued)

| Profession | Industry | Estimated size |
|---|---|---|
| Jazz musician | music | 300 |
| Light music musician | music | 4 |
| Literary translator | literature | 950 |
| Lyricist* | literature | 370 |
| Make-up artist | film | 50 |
| Mime artist | theatre | 40 |
| Music producer* | music | 100 |
| Musical theatre actor | theatre/music | 430 |
| Novelist | literature | 550 |
| Orchestra musician | music | 3,1 |
| Other dance artists* | dance | 100 |
| Other film artists* | film | 200 |
| Other literary artists* | literature | 100 |
| Other music artists* | music | 200 |
| Other theatre artists* | theatre | 150 |
| Other visual arts artists* | visual arts | 400 |
| Painter | visual arts | 1,3 |
| Painter of frescoes | visual arts | 50 |
| Performance artist** | interdisciplinary | 300 |
| Playwright | literature | 40 |
| Playwright/literary manager* | theatre | 300 |
| Poet | literature | 370 |
| Puppeteer | theatre | 270 |
| Scriptwriter | literature/film | 300 |
| Sculptor | visual arts | 300 |
| Singer | music | 600 |
| Sound director | music | 300 |
| Sound illustrator | music | 50 |
| Sound mixer | film | 200 |
| Stage designer*** | visual arts | 100 |
| Stained glass artist | visual arts | 50 |
| Theatre actor | theatre | 4,25 |
| Theatre director | theatre | 300 |
| Theatre stage designer*** | theatre / visual arts | 100 |
| Video artist | visual arts | 150 |
| Visual arts artist**** | visual arts | 400 |
| Vocalist | music | 2,8 |
| Weaver | visual arts | 30 |

*Source:* own work.[7]

## 6.3  Multi-professional index

One of the most interesting conclusions drawn from the research by Ilczuk and her team from 2018 was the multi-professional index, mentioned at the beginning of this chapter, that helped to determine other indicators. It is discussed in more detail in this section. The multi-profession index demonstrated the apparent population size of the community, which in

*Figure 6.3* Apparent and factual population size of the community (considering the common phenomenon of multi-professionalism) in Poland in 2018.

*Source:* own work.

fact is less numerous than we could assume, which is presented in Figure 6.3 and discussed in the subsequent paragraphs. The figure is a graphical representation of the scale of the multi-professionalism of the artistic community in Poland.

The multi-professionalism of the artistic community results from the fact that a great many artistic professions are practised by one individual. A good example may be one of the respondents of the survey who indicated choreography as his main profession, followed by his other professions as a costume designer, theatre dancer, and contemporary dancer.

The phenomenon of multi-professionalism of artists in the context of their non-artistic paid work was discussed by Throsby in 2010. The researcher stated that artists may in fact have other professions which are often so profitable, that they can devote the maximum amount of time to artistic work, which does not generate as much profit (Throsby

2010, p. 96). In other words, artists take other jobs to be able to afford the practising of artistic professions.

In 2011, this economist of culture together with Anita Zednik examined the situation of artists in Australia. In their research, they concentrated on two aspects. Firstly, they focused on the career paths of artists in fields not related to the arts at all, with particular reference to factors that influence the artist's decision to work outside the area of the arts. Secondly, they investigated the question of to what extent artists can use their creative skills in industries outside the core fields of culture and the arts, interpreting the results in the context of the concentric circles model of the cultural industries (Throsby and Zednik 2011). The Australian studies are then very different from the Polish surveys done by Ilczuk in 2018. The former does not include the artistic multi-professionalism of representatives of the arts, instead focusing on a Hollywood scheme of an artist-waiter.

The respondents participating in the earlier survey carried out by the Polish economist of culture and her team in 2013, as was the case with the respondents in the Australian survey, reported that they worked outside their artistic profession to a large extent. However, dancers were a specific group:

> Analysing the problem of multi-professionalism, we may state that 14.7% of women and 20% of men reported (in the CATI survey) that they performed work outside the sphere of culture not related to their main profession of an artist. Those were most frequently literary artists. This phenomenon was not reported by dancers and visual artists. The research carried out by means of in-depth interviews and focus group discussions demonstrated that dancers and visual artists very frequently used their professional expertise and skills, working on managerial positions in artistic institutions and offering educational services. (Ilczuk 2013, p. 17; translation ours)

Ilczuk also described the phenomenon which she termed 'double-professionalism.' As indicated in her research from 2015, having a second profession is a specific feature of practising the profession of an artist in Poland. This second profession is usually connected with educational work performed at schools at the higher or secondary level, cultural institutions, such as local community centres, or as part of educational projects of various types (Ilczuk 2015, pp. 73–75). As Ilczuk contends:

> This activity is, on the one hand, perceived by the interviewees as a natural combination and, on the other hand, as a possibility of staying within the sphere of creative activity even if one is performing work that belongs to this "second profession." (Ilczuk 2015, p. 73; translation ours)

Indeed, as the research showed, some artists believed that teaching has a positive impact on creativity and the second profession complements the first artistic profession. Others noted that non-artistic work, which does not concern teaching, may become too absorbing. Accordingly, the second profession becomes a kind of competition for creative activities and fulfilment in the arts (Ilczuk 2015, p. 74).

However, the survey from 2018 demonstrated a completely different feature of the labour market of artists, who still very frequently practise many professions. Yet, in this case, those were artistic professions. The phenomenon of 'artistic multi-professionalism' is somehow connected with the necessity of being artistically versatile, while working among individuals practising the arts not determined by a large demand for artistic work, which illustrates the hypothesis about the situation of artists and creators, which is inadequate to growth tendencies found in the creative economy. The survey carried out by Ilczuk and her team in 2018 shows that artists are not only engaged in work that provides them with the financing of their creative work, which was a problem discussed by Throsby. They also practise a second profession connected with education, which was discovered by Ilczuk in 2015, but above all, they are multi-artists pursuing a number of artistic professions at the same time. This situation has a bearing on the apparent population size.

The multi-professional index for the dance industry is 2.78. The result is higher than in the case of the overall index for artists in general, who on average practice 2.55 of artistic professions. As argued by Ilczuk:

> This "multi-professionalism" is a relatively common feature of the communities of artists, creators and performers … . Considering this feature of the community included in the survey, one may think that its population size is much greater than it actually is. (Ilczuk 2020, p. 13; translation ours)

## Notes

1 Some parts of this chapter were taken from Ilczuk et al. (2020).
2 The Polish abbreviations used in the table stand for the following: GUS –Statistics Poland, MF – Ministry of Finance, MPiPS – Ministry of Family, Labour and Social Policy, PISF – Polish Film Institute, IT – Theatre Institute, IMiT – National Institute of Music and Dance, SFP – Polish Filmmakers Association, PSM – Polish Association of Film Editors, PSC – Polish Society of Cinematographers, ZPAP – Union of Polish Visual Artists, ZPAV – Polish Society of the Phonographic Industry, ZAPA – Union of Audiovisual Authors and Producers, BN – National Library of Poland, ZAiKS – Society of Authors ZAiKS, STOART – STOART Society of Performers, STLu – Association of Folk Musicians, ZASP – Association of Polish Stage Artists, PFT – Polish Dance Federation, PZTan – Polish Association of Dance, ZZAP – Trade Union of Polish Actors, STOMUR – Association of Light Music Performers, STL – Polish

Literary Translators Association, SAWP – Polish Association of Performing Artists of Music and Music with Lyrics, SPAM – Association for Polish Music Artists, SPP – Association of Polish Papermakers, ZLP – Polish Writers' Union.

3 E.g. a jewellery maker, model maker, goldsmith, musical instrument builder.

4 Act on flat-rate income tax, PKD Polish Classification of Business Activities, PKWiU Polish Classification of Goods and Services.

5 The Chamber of Architects of the Republic of Poland is a form of professional self-government described in the Constitution of the Republic of Poland and a body granting permission to practise the profession.

6 Ordinance of the Minister of Culture and National Heritage of 21$^{st}$ November 2017 on establishing a national cultural institution, i.e. the National Institute of Architecture and Urban Planning.

7 *– 'new' professions suggested by the communities
** – the profession of the performance artists was shifted from the visual arts industry
*** – professions are considered separately though in fact they refer to the same profession
**** – the profession after the revision of the list, which included deleting the wrongly defined profession of 'art painter' (a profession grouping other professions)
***** – the profession not considered a main profession

## References

Ilczuk, D. (2013). Rynek pracy artystów i twórców w Polsce. *Raport z badań.* Bydgoszcz–Warszawa: Ministerstwo Kultury i Dziedzictwa Narodowego.

Ilczuk, D., Dudzik, T., Gruszka, E., & Jeran, A. (2015). *Artyści na rynku pracy.* Kraków: Wydawnictwo Attyka.

Ilczuk D., Gruszka-Dobrzyńska E., Socha Z., & Hazanowicz W. (2020). Policzone i policzeni! Artyści i artystki w Polsce, Wydawnictwo Uniwersytetu SWPS – Dom Wydawniczy Elipsa, Warszawa. Warszawa.

Throsby, D. (2001). *Economics and culture.* Cambridge University Press.

Throsby, D. (2010). Ekonomia i kultura, tłum. O. Siara, Narodowe Centrum Kultury, Warszawa.

Throsby, D., & Zednik, A. (2011). Multiple job-holding and artistic careers: Some empirical evidence. *Cultural Trends, 20*(1), 9–24.

# 7 Building cultural policies based on research

## 7.1 Support system for artists in Poland: a proposal

Cultural policies based on the welfare state model combine the state's responsibility for fostering cultural development and preserving national heritage in the context of the actual market reality and digital revolution. The contemporary cultural policy in democratic market-oriented states is understood as the deliberate and permanent interventionism of the state and local authorities in the area of culture and its industries. The main goals of cultural policy are defined as follows: preserving the cultural identity of the nation, providing equal access to culture, promoting creative activities and high-quality cultural goods and services, and achieving such diversity of the cultural offer that every social group will find something interesting in it (Benett 2001; Ilczuk 2001; Ilczuk 2002; Glondys 2010). At least one of the listed goals, i.e. the promotion of creative activity, is addressed directly to artists and creators, while the others apply to them indirectly. Naturally, depending on the chosen priority of cultural policy, the latter may be oriented more towards preserving the arts of the past or everything that is being created in the here and now. The second option is certainly more desired by artists and creators working in the contemporary world. Unfortunately, in many countries, the socio-economic situation of artists and creators and the actions of cultural policy are unsatisfactory. An example is Poland. Irrespective of their political agendas, governments in democratic Poland after 1989 did not develop any cultural policies that would have been directly addressed to artists and creators. The unreformed artistic area of culture soon began to become more and more neglected, with the professional group of artists and creators finding it increasingly difficult to claim a place in what was the reformed market world. With a remedy in mind, this situation was addressed by the research projects led by Ilczuk between 2013 and 2018.

The projects helped, above all, to determine the specifics of the given labour market and the commensurate catalogue of needs. Next, thanks to the juxtaposition of the observed deficit with potential means and

DOI: 10.4324/9781003401032-8

tools of support for artists and creators, the results served as the basis for drafting guidelines that can completely change the professional situation of artists in Poland. Let us remind the reader that the most frequent problems indicated by artists included the following: no possibility of finding full-time employment, low pay, irregular cooperation with public cultural institutions, no social security and the detrimental impact of commercialisation on culture. In most cases, those were objective problems that were directly connected with the specifics of the artists' labour market. The lack of solutions in the state cultural policy that would be beneficial for artists was also indicated, which was particularly alarming.

When the results of Ilczuk's research about the professional situation of artists in Poland were presented to international audiences, it was easy to realise that Poland is not alone regarding the observed problems. Sharing their experiences, researchers from other countries also pointed to the necessity of constantly working towards creating and improving mechanisms that can support and protect artists. They highlighted that artistic communities are diverse, whereas taking action is costly. Despite the variety of available solutions and mechanisms, there are no ideal systems. The Polish case seemed to Ilczuk, so serious that she decided to create, with the help of Karpińska, an original concept that would embody a system of support for artists and creators (Ilczuk 2017).

The presented range of solutions discussed briefly in this chapter is to a large extent based on the examples of international programmes and mechanisms. Of course, we are aware of the fact that the implementation of foreign experiences is rather unachievable since each of the proposed solutions needs to address nation-based specifics. We should also clarify, though, that we have recognised the possibility of generalising the concept proposed by Ilczuk with Karpińska and applying it in countries other than Poland. The most important feature of this concept is that one SYSTEM is built. We assume that performing artistic work should be understood as labour. This fundamental premise is the basis on which a solid and tangible support system for artists and creators should be proposed. This system settles the issue of the artist's profession, includes both social security and various forms of stimulating demand in the cultural sector, and calls for the professional monitoring and analysis of the situation of artists. The proposal for a support system was presented for the first time in the expert opinion *Reforma Kultury*, prepared by Ilczuk in cooperation with Karpińska and made available as conference material during the Polish National Conference on Culture (OKK) in 2017. The elements of the support system are presented in a simplified form in Figure 7.1.

The overall shape of the proposal is derived from the belief that only this type of complex approach to the question of support for artists may

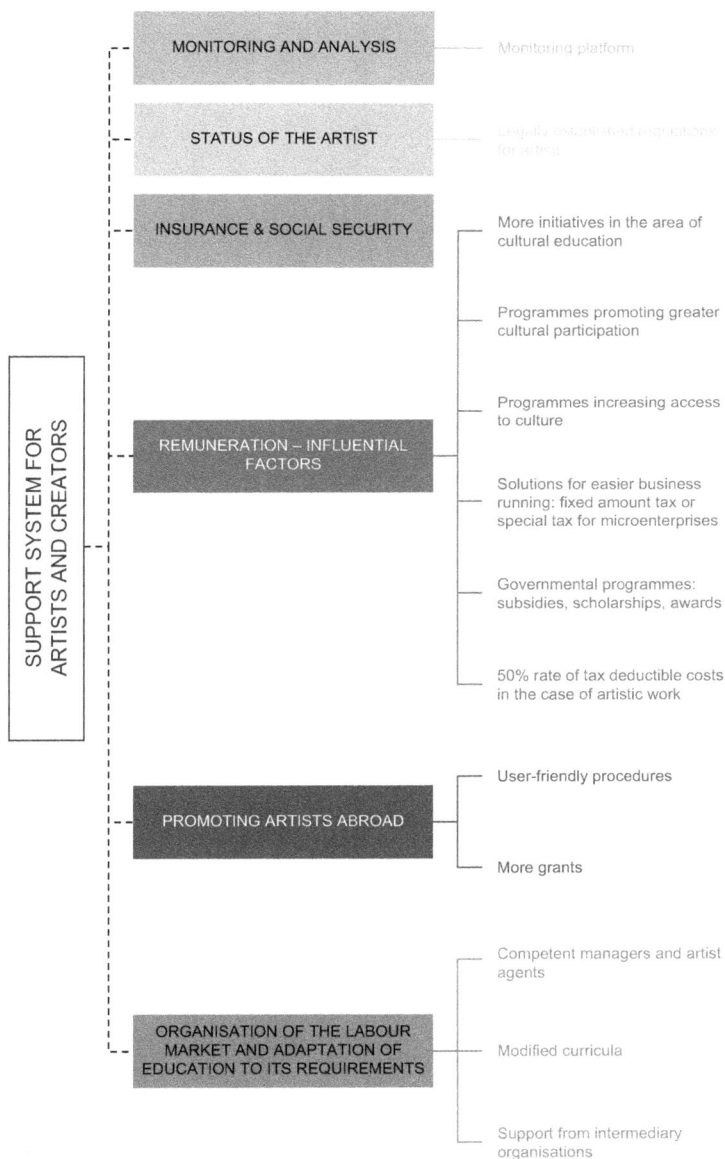

*Figure 7.1* Support system for artists and creators.
*Source:* own work based on Ilczuk 2017.

yield positive results. Therefore, all the elements of the support system resemble pieces of the same jigsaw puzzle and all are significant for the building of a support system for artists. The elements are as follows (Ilczuk et al. 2017):

- the status of the artist
- remuneration (government programmes and optional mechanisms of stimulating demand, taxes, copyright)
- insurance and social security
- the promotion of artists abroad
- the organisation of the labour market for artists and the adaptation of education to the requirements of the former
- monitoring and analysis.

It is important to note that the problem of cultural education was discussed only marginally, though, from the point of view of the situation of artists, it is considered the most significant factor stimulating demand in the cultural market. However, this problem is so complex that it would require a separate publication.

### 7.1.1 The status of the artist

From the perspective of the construction of the support system for artists, defining who can enjoy the right to solutions dedicated specifically to artists is a key problem. Criteria for qualifying may be different, ranging from purely artistic to educational or income-related. In practice, the determining of the status of the artist in the countries differs and includes both regulating the status of the artist by relevant legislation and granting the status by unions and associations of artists and creators.

Our understanding of that issue is based on an open approach in which the status of the artist would be granted not only to individuals having formal qualifications or education in a specific field. In addition to arts education, the main focus is placed on professional work, recognition in the community and participation of artistic communities in the management of the system, which would grant artists special rights resulting from the specific character of their profession.

Out of the whole proposal of a support system for artists and creators, 'the status of the artist,' which is almost a hackneyed phrase used to introduce several solutions at one time, enjoyed particular support and interest during an open public debate in Poland. The approval was so great that, initially, the status of the artist was a basis for all discussions about subsequent solutions. At first, it was also the basis on which the newly created act was founded. In the course of work and discussions, in which the risk of too normative an approach to granting the status of the artist or creator was highlighted, the concept was rejected. The only accepted concept was that of a professional artist, of which we fully approve. This concept was a point of departure and a fundamental prerequisite for the work on the support system.

### 7.1.2 Remuneration (government programmes and optional mechanisms of stimulating demand, taxes, copyright)

A sample of proposals was presented that would help to stabilise the financial situation of artists and creators.

- One of the main priorities of the state cultural policy should be an effective increase in the cultural competencies of Poles. The state should start a programme or introduce a wide scope of activities aimed at regular and extracurricular cultural education as soon as possible, as well as launch and support programmes encouraging greater participation in culture. Positive results of this proposal, which entails increased spending on culture, will become visible in a few years, but action has to be taken now.
- Well-thought-out government programmes dedicated to artists, such as various types of grants for artistic activity, scholarships and awards, are essential. They should also encompass state financial assistance in critical moments of artistic work. Not only are there no government subsidies, but also no preferential loans for artists that would enable them to start their own businesses, purchase instruments, or carry out large projects.
- About 1% of costs for building public buildings incurred by private investors should be given to the purchase of works of contemporary art. It will help support the well-being of the arts and stimulate its attendant markets.
- It is absolutely necessary to keep the 50%-level of tax-deductible costs in the case of artistic work. This type of work is time-consuming and requires special skills; in addition, the costs of materials necessary for work are so significant that making any deductions each time only increases administrative work. It is necessary to amend the tax-deduction limit on art materials, as it has a negative impact on the best artists.
- Solutions aimed at helping artists and creators to run a business should be introduced.
- The Ministry of Culture and National Heritage has been working on an amendment to the ordinance on the reprographic fee, which should amount to 1% or even 4% per tablet and computer. This, in turn, should generate about PLN 565 million (i.e. about EUR 120.73 million) for culture.[1]

### 7.1.3   *Insurance and social security*

In 2023, in Poland, there is still no effective system of health insurance and social security support dedicated to artists, which remains the main risk factor in practising the profession of an artist. Artists can pay social insurance contributions, especially to health and old-age pension insurance, on their own in accordance with general rules. This is a solution used by freelancers whose contracts do not include social security payments. Artists are required to self-register with the Social Insurance Institution (Zakład Ubezpieczeń Społecznych – ZUS) and then pay regular monthly contributions.

The first act on the pension provision of creators was introduced in 1973, although the first works began in the 1950s. After the political changes, The Ministry of Culture and National Heritage re-established the so-called Commission for Retirement of Artists and Creators by regulation in 1999. The task of this body is to recognise if a specific activity may be considered creative or artistic and, thus, to set the date of its commencement. Artists who obtain a positive opinion of the Commission may independently pay old-age pension security contributions based on their artistic work. However, this system is outdated, and so only a few artists use it.

Neither the general rules for paying social security contributions nor the Commission for Retirement of Artists and Creators are tailored to the specifics of artists' labour. They do not take into account idle time at work, which is typical of artistic professions and related to waiting for the next project. Contributions must be paid monthly and the amount varies throughout the year. What is more, a great many artists cannot afford to pay contributions themselves, as the costs place a heavy burden on them, especially considering their irregular income. A detailed proposal for solving this problem is presented in Section 6.2.

### 7.1.4   *The promotion of artists abroad*

Promoting the mobility of artists is aimed at not only helping them to reach a wider audience but also enabling them to enter a larger market. In addition, foreign promotion should allow artists to develop new contacts and participate in artistic residencies, apprenticeships or tours. For example, The Adam Mickiewicz Institute is responsible for the promotion of Polish art and Polish artists abroad. Its main task is to support participation in events taking place outside Poland. The programmes of the institute are addressed not only to artists, but also to employees of the creative sector or individuals involved in the promotion of Polish culture. However, the research results presented by Ilczuk (2013) indicate that a great many creators considered the support provided by the Adam Mickiewicz Institute as insufficient, whereas the existing application procedures were said to be too formalised.

For foreign promotion to be efficient and developed on a large scale, the number of grants available for this purpose should be increased. The diversity of needs on the part of artists and creators should be considered in this context, which will help when it comes to tailoring related programmes. First of all, procedures for granting funds for the promotion of artists abroad should be simplified. Application forms should be simple and clear in terms of their structure. The administration should be also user-friendly. It is also important to organise meetings and workshops for artists to familiarise them with the possibilities of applying for grants.

### 7.1.5 The organisation of the labour market for artists and adaptation of education to the requirements of the former

The level of the organisation of the labour market for artists and creators in Poland is low, with a great many artists not availing themselves of the support of artistic agencies. However, this is caused not only by the high costs of their services, but also by the lack of confidence in their competencies. Moreover, during their education, artists are not prepared to stay mobile within the market. They lack numerous entrepreneurial skills.

It is important to educate trustworthy and competent artist managers and agents, whose presence in the Polish market is still not visible. Currently, only the highest-paid artists can afford their services. Managers and agents should know relevant legal regulations and market rules as well as be able to support creators in obtaining grants and other administrative activities.

It is also crucial to modify the curricula of arts faculties. In addition to compulsory courses in the chosen field of study, curricula should include a component that prepares future artists to act in the reality of the market. Young creators must learn the principles of entrepreneurship, i.e. they need to know how to run their own businesses, cooperate with businesses or start a job. Students should be provided with information on where to seek support and what grant opportunities are available to them.

### 7.1.6 Monitoring and analysis

We cannot manage effectively if our knowledge of a specific area is insufficient. We usually have reservations about cultural statistics. However, the institutional part of it is still the object of regular interest of statistical offices, no matter how imperfect this interest may be, and of qualitative research. Unfortunately, in the case of artists, statistical data are rather limited. In fact, the only information available in public collections of statistics concerns pupils, students and the graduates of art schools. Data on employees of the cultural sectors are presented as an aggregate, which means that artists are not considered an individual group. As a result, we often do not even know how many artists there are, how much they earn or what their professional situation is. We are unable to estimate the costs of planned solutions. The lowest expectations in this regard can only be an orderly organisation of quantitative research on artists conducted as part of keeping official statistics. What should follow is a commission given by public authorities to research institutions for a regular report prepared based on quantitative and qualitative research into the professional situation of artists every four years. A good solution would also be the creation of a platform for monitoring the socio-economic situation of employees of the cultural and creative industries in Poland, including artists and creators.

### 7.2    Towards an act on the professional artist

In working materials regarding the cooperation of the Creative Economy Research Center of SWPS University with the socio-economic environment, created to report academic achievements in 2021, Ilczuk and Karpińska wrote:

> *The fact that cultural policy in Poland after 1989 has been focused around institutions and the system of financing programmes and projects has led to a situation in which culture and the arts have become detached from their creators, whereas artists and performers have become absent from the whole system.*

Presenting the proposal to create a support system for artists and creators, Ilczuk and Karpińska drew attention to the need for an open public debate among artistic communities, and, then, to revise the findings within a limited team of experts, including experts in the field of economics, law and management. Before implementing the solutions, it is necessary to apply them as pilot projects, preferably run by local authorities. It is also important to ensure constant cooperation with all stakeholders of the new system, including artistic communities, local authorities or civic organisations, as well as to promote new solutions and to pass a relevant act, i.e. a legal regulation reflecting the proposal.

The published outcomes led by Ilczuk's series of research presenting the situation of artists in the Polish labour market against the international perspective have contributed to the fact that the socio-economic situation of artists and creators became the main topic of debate during the Polish National Conference on Culture (OKK) in 2017, mentioned in the previous section. The conference brought together the artistic community and created space for discussions about the situation of artists and creators. It was the OKK conference along with the commitment of the community that led to the Minister of Culture and National Heritage reaching a momentous decision to start working on legislation covering the rights of professional artists. The minister created a group of independent experts led by the 'engineer of the act,' i.e. the director of the Fryderyk Chopin Institute, Artur Szklener PhD. The group included also Professor Ilczuk, who was supported by Anna Karpińska.

The first difficulty encountered by the group was a general lack of knowledge about the population size of the community that the new legislation would cover. It made financial calculations concerning future solutions generally impossible. Therefore, a decision was made to carry out research into the population size of artists and creators, to be conducted by Ilczuk at the CBnGK of SWPS University research centre. The team developed new methodological tools which helped to estimate the population size with high precision. In addition to determining the population size of the community, which made it possible to estimate the number of individuals covered by the new regulations and the costs associated with them, and to recognise the need for special support in terms of social security, the research also looked at forms of employment and the earnings of artists. It also helped to determine the scale of non-contractual work, classified as an informal economy, which, together with data on the income of the research population, became the basis for developing detailed provisions of the newly proposed act.

However, this was not the only research that supported the legislation process. At various stages of the process, the expert group used data about the situation of artists that have been gathered by Professor Ilczuk since 2013, when she conducted the first survey about the situation of artists in the labour market (i.e. the Warsaw-Bydgoszcz survey). Information about the socio-economic status of artists was included in documents necessary for the implementation of the new legislation, including the document providing the reasons for the introduction of solutions (*Informacje o przyczynach i potrzebie wprowadzenia rozwiązań planowanych w projekcie*) and another one justifying the Act, which is an attachment to the bill (*Uzasadnienie ustawy*). While drafting the bill, the expert group referred also to the expert report by Ilczuk in cooperation with. The data from the mentioned research projects was also used in information and promotional materials regarding the proposed solutions. The concept of a system of support for artists described by Ilczuk (2017) and presented during one of the debates of the Polish National Conference on Culture became pivotal to future discussions on the status and rights of artists.

### 7.2.1  *Proposed bill on the professional artist*

According to the bill on professional artists of 1 June 2022 (registered under number UD208 in the register of legislative procedures), relevant rights will be enjoyed by graduates of higher art schools, ballet schools and schools of circus art following their submission of an application for the recognition of their qualifications no later than five years after obtaining the relevant diploma, as well as by artists and creators whose artistic achievements will have been confirmed by a representative organisation. In other words, achievements will have to be assessed by associations or professional unions representative for a specific artistic profession, i.e. they will have a membership at the level of at least 10% of artists working in a given area. In addition to confirming artistic achievements, the role of representative organisations will be to appoint and elect members of the Council of the Polish Chamber of Artists, a QUANGO-type organisation, whose main goal will be to manage the support system for professional artists. Two-thirds of the members of the council will be representatives of artistic organisations, and one-third will be made up of the representatives of state authorities.

The confirmation of artistic achievements will not be based on qualitative assessments of the language of the arts. An artist wishing to obtain or maintain the status of a professional artist (the confirmation will have to be performed every three years until status is consolidated, i.e. an individual has worked for the appropriate number of years as an artist) will have to submit a statement on the revenue obtained from artistic work as an appropriate percentage of all earnings. Revenue thresholds included in the bill were determined based on the results of the estimation of the population size described in Chapter 5 and differentiated depending on the profession. The official revenue threshold list will be published as an ordinance of the Minister of Culture and National Heritage after the bill has been passed and the new Act comes into force. If the artist is not able to prove the required level of revenue, a representative organisation will be entitled to confirm the achievements according to different terms and conditions.

Applying for the professional artist status will be voluntary. The status will secure

> the right to pay contributions to social security, health insurance and the Labour Fund in the amount of total contributions set for the insured and the payer, calculated for the minimum wage (in 2022 it is PLN 1,223.26 per month) [approximately EUR 261.38]. Professional artists whose average monthly revenue in the previous calendar year was lower than 80% of the average remuneration in the national economy (in 2021 it amounted to PLN 5,682.97) [approximately EUR 1,214.31] is granted a subsidy for contributions in the amount of 20% to 80% of the contributions. (*Artysta Zawodowy*- https://artystazawodowy.pl)

Moreover, in accordance with the bill, a Professional Artist ID Card will be created, which will be aimed at identifying professional artists and guaranteeing them the rights granted by the Ministry of Culture and other entities, such as institutions or local authorities. This solution will help to create special offers for cardholders, such as free admission to cultural institutions, discounts dedicated to this professional group or special offers in the area of specialist medical care.

Subsidies for social security and health insurance contributions granted to professional artists will be financed from the Support Fund for Professional Artists supervised by the Director of the Polish Chamber of Artists. This fund will be partially financed by payments collected as a reprographic fee, which is a form of compensation for copying works within the framework of private use, thanks to which we can share music, books or films with family and friends for free. The reprographic fee is not a Polish solution, as within the European Union it is regulated in Directive 2001/29/EC. The reprographic, or reproduction fee, as it is referred to in the directive, is collected for each device used for copying and playing works covered by intellectual property rights, for example, computers, tablets or smartphones. In Poland, the last update of the list of devices and storage media used to record works for which a reprographic fee is collected took place about ten years ago. The list includes copiers, scanners, fax machines, CD players, tape recorders, etc. However, new technologies such as smartphones are still absent from the list. As the newly created Act will include the financing of artists' support, based to a large extent on this fee, a debate centred around the updating of this list has begun. Worth noting here is the fact that these initiatives have been resisted by the lobby of hi-tech producers, who started a campaign against the changes and the proposed Act on the rights of a professional artist.

Introducing the Act on the rights of a professional artist will lead to a situation where 42,000 individuals from the 60 thousandth group of artists and creators, who up till now were not able to afford social security payments, will be covered by the scheme. As indicated in the brochure about legal regulations for artists (Artysta Zawodowy 2022), the Social Insurance Institution, the Labour Fund and the National Health Fund will receive additional contributions of an annual value of approximately PLN 415 million (about EUR 88.67 million). The act developed based on the research will allow professional artists to calculate social security and health insurance contributions, taking into account the specific character of their profession.

### 7.2.2 *A difficult road to the implementation of the research results in the context of cultural policy*

The working process on the Act on professional artists has been ongoing in Poland since 2017, when the Fryderyk Chopin Institute, following the initiative of the Minister of Culture and National Heritage, organised the already-mentioned National Conference on Culture. Several structural solutions were proposed, covering such issues as the definition of a professional artist and the rights resulting from it as well as solutions related to tax advantages, social security and health insurance benefits, old-age pension security and pre-retirement benefits. The problems of financing culture were also taken into account; accordingly, solutions that would not significantly strain the state budget were also considered.

The final effect should be highlighted: the new Act will be innovative and democratic. This will result not only from the process of creating the proposed bill, but also from the text itself and implications resulting directly from its content. First of all, the solutions presented in the bill are based on the highest standards of research. Considering the context of the history of Poland and its communist legacy, the project authors endeavoured to ensure that the Act would not allow for making arbitrary decisions.

Work on the implementation of this modern and long-awaited system that will give artists, e.g. access to the social security system, which is an important human right, has been continuing for five years. This is so because of many reasons. However, one of the main reasons for the legislative delay has been the strength and effectiveness of the hi-tech lobby, which, suddenly, started to fight against the updating of the list of entities covered by the reprographic fee, which was to be the basis for financing new solutions. In the middle of this fight, artists have been paradoxically left out. As a result, the main focus has been shifted to the consequences of the method of financing the Act, which, according to the producers' lobby, will have a negative impact on the prices of devices, such as smartphones, tablets or computers. A very aggressive campaign against the Act was launched, aimed at discouraging public opinion from the proposed solutions. On one side, there is the revenue interest of multi-million corporations producing IT equipment, and on the other, we have a relatively small (fewer than 60,000 individuals) professional and social group: this polarity has informed political decisions and also swayed artists and creators.

However, there are many other burning issues connected with potential amendments to the bill, particularly those coming from the Ministry of Finance. As a result, artists in Poland are continuing to have to make do without support. The first issue is the lack of common knowledge about cultural policy among the majority of artists, which, in turn, means that cooperation between artistic communities and politicians, who do not know the specifics of the artists' labour market, becomes problematic. Inequalities, indicated in the research by Ilczuk and her team, as well as internal conflicts among artistic communities, are also common. This has all been caused by different expectations across various professional groups, and here we must also acknowledge generational differences.

Another constant challenge is the lack of confidence in systematic solutions, which the community perceives as governmental. The lengthy legislative process was meant to ensure equal access to participation in the pre-drafting process through consultations with the community and, in turn, to ensure the creation of a 'tailor-made' system rather than a politicised and populist one. However, the attempts at politicization of the arts and subordination of artists have led to disengagement among members of the artistic community, despite the benefits which would accrue to them. These issues, related to despondency and a loss of faith in the process, were articulated by many representatives of the artistic community in the research of Ilczuk in 2018 and 2020.

Still, the fight for the introduction of support for artists has been on. A good illustration of the lingering hope of artists and creators may be the campaigns of some artistic organisations or individual artists as well as the campaign of the Fryderyk Chopin Institute, which publicly campaigns against the difficult socio-economic situation of artists, drawing attention to the specific character of their work. Thanks to this, social awareness of this relatively small community is constantly increasing.

Another sign of re-emergent voices came with a letter sent at the beginning of 2023 to the Prime Minister of the Republic of Poland, Mateusz Morawiecki. The authors of the letter, so far left unanswered, were Dominik Skoczyk, the director of both the Polish Filmmakers Association and the Union of Audiovisual Authors and Producers, and Piotr Kulczycki from the Union of Independent Theatres. The contents of the letter had been discussed and agreed with several other organisations, including the Association of Authors ZAIKS. It was signed by a great many individuals involved in the fight for the implementation of the act on professional artists. While we are writing this book, parliamentary elections are coming soon in Poland (15 October 2023).In the current campaign, the bill for professional artists has become a political issue and electoral card for opposition parties.

In this chapter, we have verified our initial hypotheses set out in the introduction regarding the area of cultural policy. One of them reads as follows:

*The professional situation of artists and creators is not adequate to the observed tendencies of development, according to which culture and its industries have been considered a significant component of the creative economy, and accordingly, a new area of investment, a source of creativity and innovation.*

The research results clearly show that in a globalised world, the role of the CCS, the cultural and creative industries and industries related to them is constantly growing, contributing to economic growth and an increase in standards of living (see also Deloitte report 2021), then the labour market for artists and creators cannot be left as it is. The conditions for performing artistic work are crucial for development processes of the CCS.

This is an important conclusion drawn from our analysis. It also touches on the broader issue of state interventionism in the sectors of the creative economy. Let us recall at this point what our research hypothesis on interventionism in the field of artistic work was:

*Influencing both the supply and demand side of the labour market of artists and creators by means of instruments of support offered by the state, local authorities, non-governmental and private institutions contributes to greater growth of the creative economy.*

## Note

1 EUR 1 = PLN 4.68 according to the average exchange rate of the National Bank of Poland in 2022.

## References

Artysta Zawodowy. (2022). Prawo dla artystów w pigułce. Warsaw.
Bennett, T. (2001). Differing diversities. *Cultural Policy and Cultural Diversity*. Brussels: Council of Europe Publishing.
Glondys, D. (2010). Europejska Stolica Kultury. Miejsce kultury w Unii Europejskiej, Attyka, Kraków.
Ilczuk, D. (2001). Cultural citizenship. Civil society and cultural policy in Europe, BOEKMANstudies/CIRCLE. Amsterdam.
Ilczuk, D. (2002). Polityka Kulturalna w Społeczeństwie Obywatelskim, Wydawnictwo Uniwersytetu Jagiellońskiego, Kraków.
Ilczuk, D. (2013). Rynek pracy artystów i twórców w Polsce. Raport z badań, Bydgoszcz–Warszawa: Ministerstwo Kultury i Dziedzictwa Narodowego.
Ilczuk, D., in cooperation with Karpińska A., Noga M. (2017). Reforma kultury w Polsce, Ogólnopolska Konferencja Kultury, Warszawa.
Ilczuk, D., Karpińska, A., & Stano-Strzałkowska, S. (2017). Wsparcie dla twórców i artystów, Perspektywa Międzynarodowa. https://nck.pl/upload/ attachments/319282/Wsparcie%20dla%20twórców%20i%20artystów.%20 Perspektywa%20międzynarodowa.pdf

# 8 Conclusions

This book is a result of analytical and research work done together by three cultural economists – the experienced one and the two at the beginning of their academic careers. Their mutual analysis was based on the results of extensive research projects into the artists' labour market initiated and supervised by Professor Dorota Ilczuk between 2012 and 2022. The book encapsulates the multifaceted issue of artists in the labour market, examined from various angles. Firstly, it is situated in the context of widely recognised knowledge from the field of cultural economics. Secondly, thinking about constantly changing cultural policies, market rules and the generic changes in the world – mainly, but not only for artists. Thirdly, from the time perspective – the research projects run by Ilczuk were undertaken over a decade.

Following the aims indicated in the introduction, the scientific work on that book belongs to a broad area of research into the development of the creative economy around the world; emphasising the significance of artistic work and the labour market for artists and creators in this context. Let us move on to a summary of the results of our analytical efforts.

Artistic work is an important, if not the most important, factor in the production of symbolic goods and services created in the sectors of the creative economy. Thanks to a series of studies run by Ilczuk in past years, we were able to determine the scale and specifics of the professional situation of artists and creators, taking into account gender contexts and exceptional situations such as the COVID-19 pandemic. Apart from having a large amount of measurable, quantitative data coming from different research projects, the personal opinions of artists were also considered. This helped us to accurately identify various gaps in the government policies relating to both the supply side (schools and art education) and the demand side (the scale of direct support for artists, tax reliefs, the level of cultural education in general schooling) of the artists' labour market. In response to that picture, we have shown an original proposal for a system of support for artists and creators, which was

DOI: 10.4324/9781003401032-9

subsequently used in the legislative considerations focused on the profession of an artist. Thus, the data presented in the book not only has informative dimensions but also shows the actual application potential and outcomes of the research.

The results of our findings into the specifics of the labour market of artists and creators are in line with the trends currently recognised by researchers studying the same subject. These trends include a strong deregulation of the market, where the situation of artists is characterised by uncertainty around commission and irregular income, which may sometimes reach a very high level, but is not always correlated with artistic success. The specific situation of artists in Poland means that no solutions have been presented to address social security concerns, in particular health and old-age pension insurance. Our success has been to show a new and more in-depth perspective of the problem. Therefore, our conclusions include those which, thanks to their original and innovative nature, have added a new value to research into the labour market of artists. Below, we present three conclusions worth highlighting.

The first one comes from the research that may be considered one of the most important, i.e. pioneering project, which was aimed at estimating the number of working artists and creators in Poland. Having used an original method of estimating the population size displayed in Chapter 6, the number of artists, creators and performers at the level of almost 60,000 individuals was estimated in Poland in 2018. The number was surprising to both the researchers, artists and creators. It was commonly believed that the number was lower than had been expected. Its accuracy was explained by the mysterious multi-professional index described in Chapter 6, too. Finally, the important conclusion drawn from the study is then as follows:

*The population size of professional artists and creators is only apparent. In reality, the population is smaller than it is commonly believed. This is related to the fact that one representative of the arts practises several professions. This is reflected in the phenomenon of multi-professionalism calculated by the multi-professional index.*

It was the phenomenon of multi-professionalism observed during the research on the population size of artists and creators and the calculated multi-professional index that guaranteed the accuracy of the results obtained. At the same time, it helped us to realise that the community of working artists is, in fact, a relatively small social group. On the one hand, it means fairly low costs of their support, but on the other hand, it means a limited significance of this group in the context of the election strategies of politicians.

The second conclusion had been drawn in the course of analysing the conditions for artistic work; this followed to indicate differences across this state of affairs, which to date have not been highlighted. That is why we believe it is important to note that:

*A misconception in any analyses of artists and of their labour market would be perceiving their socio-economic situation as homogeneous. Apart from factors specific to artistic work, such as irregular and low income or the lack of guaranteed old-age pension benefits, the socio-economic situation varies because they of their belonging to a specific professional group and practising a specific profession; or because of gender differences.*

In other words, the concern about being a member of the precariat is not observed in the case of a ballet dancer employed at the National Ballet and Opera, but it seems commonplace in the case of a painter or writer. On the other hand, in the case of a ballet dancer, the main concern is connected with a high risk of injury and a short period of professional activity. Similarly, there are a great many inequalities among women and men within artistic professions, related mainly to the question of professional paths, gender pay gaps, weekly working hours, as well as differences between education and active years on the market between men and women. Moreover, abnormal events and unusual circumstances, such as pandemics, disproportionately affect female and male artists, as well as representatives of various artistic professions and fields.

Our final conclusion, probably the most significant one, would be drawn in the course of the analysis of our research object from the perspective of a threefold structure – **the artists' labour market – creative sectors – cultural policy**, which creates a particular **triangular model;** considered by us as an added value of our analyses.

These three areas are connected by an inseparable bond. Firstly, the professional situation of artists and creators is largely determined by the labour market in the creative sectors. Without artists, industries such as music or film would not function. It is artistic work that is the basis of or a contribution to the employment of many individuals and the production of the final value, which, in turn, generates profit. Secondly, business does not always support free artistic development, being guided by a desire to maximise profit and monetise cultural goods, which often does not provide stable employment. Many artists work under a contract for work or a contract of service. And therefore, thirdly, the role of cultural policy is to look at artistic work from a more sensitive perspective; to support the development of creative activity and non-commercial initiatives.

One of the main goals of cultural policy is also to monitor the development of culture and the arts in the country; and to make this development possible by launching various programmes, offering grants, scholarships and awards, promoting and creating systems of support for artists. It is cultural policy that is also responsible for shaping demand for cultural goods by way of a well-developed cultural education that promotes cultural participation. At the same time, without artists, there would be neither a creative economy nor a cultural policy. After all, artists are responsible for the symbolic aspect of cultural goods, staying at the top of our triangular model. We believe it is very important to recognise this connectedness and its strength.

Thus, a significant change in one element of this figure will naturally influence the other elements. It is both a strength and a weakness of the whole jigsaw. The introduction of solutions, such as the legislation on professional artists, and a regulation of the labour market of artists and creators, will bring about changes in the creative sectors, supported by the greater bargaining power of artists, whose socio-economic situation will become stable, which, in turn, will allow them to reject unprofitable commissions.

Moreover, let us emphasise the fact that our research proves that all the elements of the triangular model lack regular and professional monitoring and analysis, which should become part of a broader system of solutions that will have a positive impact on the artists' labour market or sectors of the creative economy.

The original contribution of our research consists in showing the generic, comprehensive view of the subject and the process of the empirical results' implementation. The presented method of using the research outcomes and the current legislative process focused on professional artists in Poland are both good examples of the importance of this research for the socio-economic environment, in particular, for shaping the current cultural policy. We may, then, feel confident and say that the goals set out in the introduction, both in terms of research and application, have been fully achieved. As for the aim to disseminate the results, we can only hope that such a transition will take place. Nevertheless, we have expended much effort to explain the importance of understanding the relations between the creative economy, the labour market of artists, and cultural policies in a series of long-term research paths led by Ilczuk. Figure 7.2 offers a graphic illustration of this effort, referring as it does to a similar figure presented in the introduction (see Figure 8.1) to this monograph, but it presents a new component connected with the impact our research has had on the socio-economic environment (Figure 8.1).

Now, let's think about what lies ahead. The future economy will be based on the connection between creativity and technology. Creativity is considered the most important competence of future employees. The contribution of the creative economy sectors to the development of soft skills and creativity looks set to become even more critical in the era of artificial intelligence (AI) and workplace automation. Even if computers and robots take over routine tasks, humans will still have great opportunities by combining artistic, creative, technical, social and emotional skills that are resistant to automation. Therefore, it will

## RESEARCH

## IMPACT OF RESEARCH

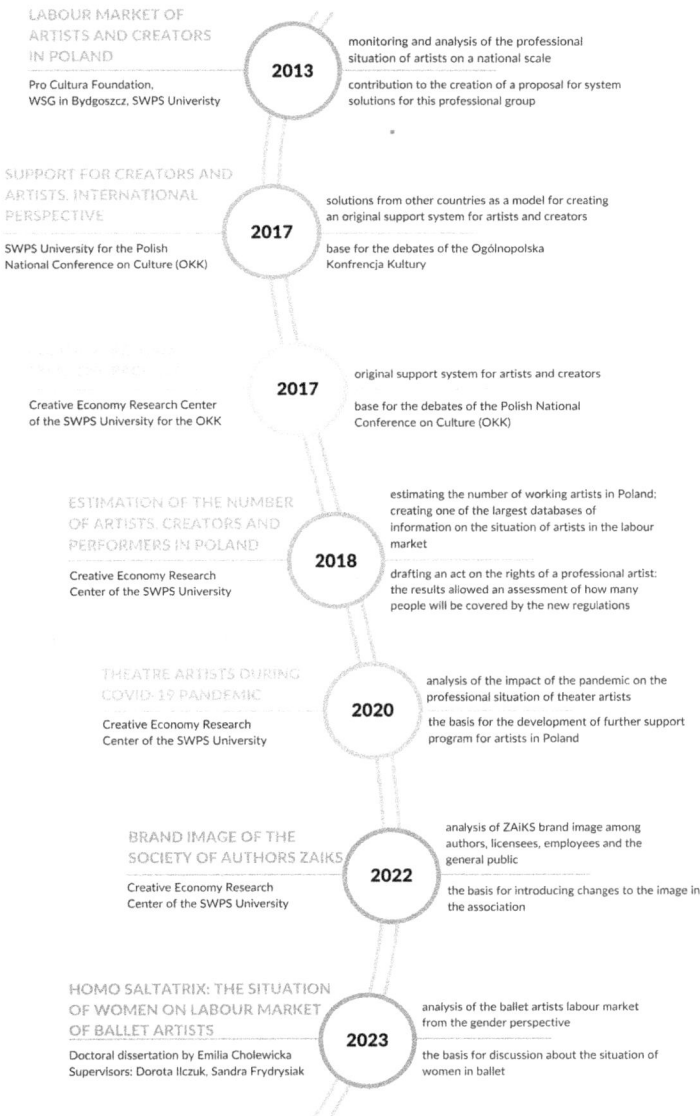

LABOUR MARKET OF
ARTISTS AND CREATORS
IN POLAND

**2013**

monitoring and analysis of the professional
situation of artists on a national scale

Pro Cultura Foundation,
WSG in Bydgoszcz, SWPS Univeristy

contribution to the creation of a proposal for system
solutions for this professional group

SUPPORT FOR CREATORS AND
ARTISTS, INTERNATIONAL
PERSPECTIVE

**2017**

solutions from other countries as a model for creating
an original support system for artists and creators

SWPS University for the Polish
National Conference on Culture (OKK)

base for the debates of the Ogólnopolska
Konfrencja Kultury

**2017**

original support system for artists and creators

Creative Economy Research Center
of the SWPS University for the OKK

base for the debates of the Polish National
Conference on Culture (OKK)

ESTIMATION OF THE NUMBER
OF ARTISTS, CREATORS AND
PERFORMERS IN POLAND

**2018**

estimating the number of working artists in Poland;
creating one of the largest databases of
information on the situation of artists in the labour
market

Creative Economy Research
Center of the SWPS University

drafting an act on the rights of a professional artist:
the results allowed an assessment of how many
people will be covered by the new regulations

THEATRE ARTISTS DURING
COVID-19 PANDEMIC

**2020**

analysis of the impact of the pandemic on the
professional situation of theater artists

Creative Economy Research
Center of the SWPS University

the basis for the development of further support
program for artists in Poland

BRAND IMAGE OF THE
SOCIETY OF AUTHORS ZAIKS

**2022**

analysis of ZAiKS brand image among
authors, licensees, employees and the
general public

Creative Economy Research
Center of the SWPS University

the basis for introducing changes to the image in
the association

HOMO SALTATRIX: THE SITUATION
OF WOMEN ON LABOUR MARKET
OF BALLET ARTISTS

**2023**

analysis of the ballet artists labour market
from the gender perspective

Doctoral dissertation by Emilia Cholewicka
Supervisors: Dorota Ilczuk, Sandra Frydrysiak

the basis for discussion about the situation of
women in ballet

*Figure 8.1.* Research and its implementation.

*Source:* own work.

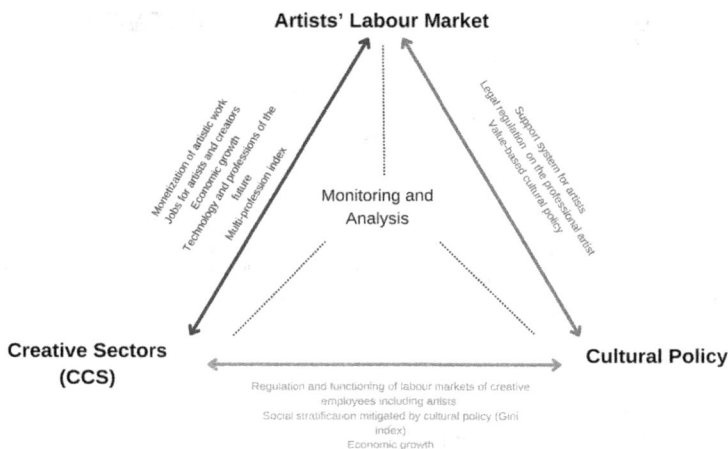

*Figure 8.2.* The artists' labour market – creative sectors – cultural policy triangular model.

*Source:* own work.

be necessary to systematically and wisely support the functioning of all the elements, or rather all the entities of the creative economy sectors, especially those directly creating symbolic capital that is a distinctive feature of the creative economy (Figure 8.2).

Our analyses owe much to the tenacity and passion of Professor Dorota Ilczuk for cultural economics and, mainly, the subject of artists' situation and their lives. However, one of the main shortcomings of the research may be a subjective bias of one particular researcher. Indeed, it has been our dream to make this research part of a larger whole or a platform for monitoring and analysing the socio-economic situation of employees of the cultural and creative industries in Poland, including artists and creators. The method developed and positively used in the 2018 research provides a tool for this dream to come true, and continuously be dreamed by a wider group of cultural economists.

Delving into the intricacies of the artistic community's work has been a fascinating and productive endeavour. This community holds a unique allure for researchers from diverse fields. As cultural economists, we were particularly impressed by the resilience of artists, who, despite financial challenges, thrive on their talent and creativity. These attributes carry substantial potential for driving economic growth, fostering innovation, and promoting inclusivity and social equity.

It's crucial to highlight that ensuring financial stability for artists has wide-ranging societal benefits. Positive efforts in this direction will not only enhance cultural development but also contribute to the advancement of civilization and social well-being. Let's hope for balanced and prudent interactions within the examined triangular model encompassing the creative economy, the artist labour market, and cultural policies.

# Index

Note: *Italicized* and **bold** page numbers refer to figures and tables. Page numbers followed by "n" refer to notes.

For Product Safety Concerns and Information please contact our EU
representative GPSR@taylorandfrancis.com
Taylor & Francis Verlag GmbH, Kaufingerstraße 24, 80331 München, Germany